A Red State

of Mind

Also by Nancy French

South Pacific Journal
(with David French)

A Red State of Mind

of Mind

How a Catfish Queen Reject
Became a Liberty Belle

NANCY FRENCH

**CENTER
STREET** ®

NEW YORK   BOSTON   NASHVILLE

Author's note: These stories are true, although the names have been changed—with a few notable exceptions. Rene, of course, demanded I use her real name because she wants to be famous and an expert on *Oprah* about how to survive bipartisan friendships. Rebecca also let me use her name to make up for the whole stroller bomb squad incident. Plus, I used the real names of my family . . . I'm actually married to David, although in the book I seriously understated his love for paintball.

Center Street®
Hachette Book Group USA
1271 Avenue of the Americas, New York, NY 10020

Visit our Web site at www.centerstreet.com.

Center Street is a division of Hachette Book Group USA. The Center Street name and logo are trademarks of Hachette Book Group USA.

Printed in the United States of America

First Edition: October 2006

10   9   8   7   6   5   4   3   2   1

Library of Congress Cataloging-in-Publication Data

French Nancy.
    A Red State of mind : how a catfish queen reject became a liberty belle / Nancy French. — 1st ed.
        p. cm.
    Summary: "Nancy French, columnist for 'The Philadelphia Daily News' and a former beauty queen from red-state Tennessee, tells what it's like to live in blue-state New York in this humorous memoir"—Provided by publisher.
    ISBN-13: 978-1-931722-88-9
    ISBN-10: 1-931722-88-9
    1. French, Nancy. 2. Authors, American—21st century—Biography. 3. Women journalists—Pennsylvania—Philadelphia—Biography. 4. United States—Politics and government—2001—Humor. 5. Political culture—New York (State)—Humor. 6. Conservatism—United States—Humor. 7. Liberalism—United States—Humor. I. Title.
    PS3556.R43Z46 2006
    813'.54—dc22
    [B]   2006011587

To the American military,
who battles the enemies of freedom
so that I can battle dirty dishes,
writer's block, and the overconsumption of
chocolate—peanut-butter ice cream.
And to David,
who will go to basic training this year
at the age of thirty-seven.

Acknowledgments

Thank you to:

D. J. Snell, who dreamed this up after laughing at my e-mails.

Bob Anderson, who was a marine at fifteen and
a college graduate at fifty.
Betty Anderson, who wiped noses and patted behinds
to pay for my college.
Amy Westerman, who can do virtually anything.
Mary Kate Anderson, who believed me when I told her
pickles tasted like spaghetti.
Camille French, who defied a principal.
Austin French, who survived the hospital.
James A. and Belinda French, who turned us into farmers.

Shannon Martin, who tackled the tough issues of
life over coffee and quiche.
Rebecca Scott, whose stroller almost got me arrested.
Virginia Camille Waller, who inspired more than my
daughter's name.
Stephen Prewitt, who knew I was skipping class but let me
talk to David anyway.

Shaunti Feldhahn, who witnessed many of the events
in this book.
Rene Weiner, who caused them.

Thank you to the people in the cities I've called home:

Paris, Tennessee,
New York, New York,
Georgetown, Kentucky,
Nashville, Tennessee,
Ithaca, New York,
Lexington, Kentucky,
Philadelphia, Pennsylvania,
Columbia, Tennessee,

who provided the material for this book.

Thank you to:
Duane Swierczynski, of the Philadelphia *City Paper*,
who owes me a quarter,
and
Michael Schefer, of the *Philadelphia Daily News*,
to whom I owe lunch.

Thank you to everyone at Time Warner Book Group,
including Maureen Egen; Rolf Zettersten; Chip MacGregor;
Lori Quinn; Penina Sacks; Martha Schwartz;
Kelly Berry, who made conference calls
as pleasant as afternoon tea; and Chris Min Park, who made
me look good in more ways than one.

And especially David French, whose spontaneity and courage
seduce me still.

Contents

I truly believe that if the red states and blue states made a sincere effort to get to know each other, they would discover that, beneath their surface differences, there are a lot of deep, underlying differences.

—*Dave Barry*

We consider ourselves bicoastal if you consider the Mississippi River one of the coasts.

—*Ron Albertson, in* Waiting for Guffman

Introduction

ONCE, IN A fit of ambition, I teased my hair, put on blue satin and pink eye shadow, and entered the Catfish Queen beauty pageant—unaware that my lack of poise, fish knowledge, and cleavage would present serious obstacles in my quest for the coveted crown. Every third week in April, seventy thousand people converge on my hometown of Paris, Tennessee, for the World's Biggest Fish Fry. It was probably best I lost the contest, since the Catfish Queen had many responsibilities I couldn't have mastered—including serving fish in the Fish Tent (where six tons are consumed in one week) and maintaining perfect posture while perched atop a slow-moving convertible during the climactic parade down Eastwood Street.

The biggest draw of the parade was the celebrity grand marshal, for example, Porter Wagoner or Patsy Cline's third-grade teacher. And schools were dismissed so we could walk up and down the road and shoot Silly String at the floats. The Fish Fry Festival gave us a sense of being a part of something bigger than our typical small-town life, but when it was over, farmers went back to their tobacco, kids went back to school, and committees started work on next year's floats.

Yet even after the tourists left, you never felt lonely in Paris. Just a casual drive through the town was a community experience, requiring the following unspoken rules of etiquette not taught in driver's ed. Obviously, the cardinal rule was to wave at passing vehicles (not a formal Queen Elizabeth but just a relaxed steering wheel salute) whether or not you knew the other driver. Most of the time, you did.

Just as important was the rule for funeral processions. As in most places, police cars escorted a meandering line of cars to the cemetery after a funeral. In Paris, however, the driver of any car that came upon the procession pulled off the road, put on his hazard lights, and bowed his head slightly as it passed. The ultimate measure of a life well lived was how many miles of traffic you could shut down on your way to the Pearly Gates.

Of course, if you passed a police officer hiding in a speed trap, you dutifully flashed your headlights on and off to alert oncoming traffic—the vehicular equivalent of the Golden Rule.

And lastly, a four-way stop in Tennessee was the perfect opportunity to demonstrate one's Christianity. The driver who arrived first at the intersection, though entitled by law to go first, often motioned "after you" to the other driver. This made four-way stops long, ambiguous pageants of humility and thankful waves (as opposed to the four-way collisions that any such traffic configuration causes in New York).

In other words, people in Paris watched out for each other well before anyone articulated the notion of it taking a village.

It was also before we knew airliners could be used as missiles and before anyone had heard of Columbine.

Perhaps in retrospect, it *was* a little odd that my junior high actually encouraged firearm use by replacing seventh-grade science class with a mandatory hunter's safety course. I vividly remember our football coach standing in front of the class with an array of rifles and shotguns, showing us how to take lethal shots from the deer stand and how to gut deer properly. We even had field trips to a shooting range, where I earned the distinction of being the best marksman in my junior high school. Three skeet. No misses. And I'd never shot a gun before.

This was much more practical than dissecting a frog, since we students had arsenals in our homes that made Saddam look like a beatnik (and we could dissect frogs in our own backyards). It never dawned on me that I was a redneck. Even when my friends and I entertained ourselves by going cow tipping— which involves stealthily sneaking up on sleeping cows and slamming into them until they tip over—I just figured we were participating in a classic American pastime. (Yes, cows sleep standing up and have a terrible sense of balance. Cow tipping is illegal since, sadly, some cows can't recover from the sudden shock.)

Luckily I had plenty of opportunity to ask God to forgive me. In Paris, churches were packed on Sunday mornings, and smoky bars were packed on Saturday nights—sometimes by the same folk. On weekday mornings, the retired men sat for hours in local diners smoking Marlboros and analyzing Tennessee football. Younger men were judged by the size of their trucks and their skill at fixing them. Women, on the other hand, were kept busy by hairdos that defied gravity and required architectural skills surpassing those of the builders of the Eiffel Tower—a sixty-foot replica of which was the pride of our county.

Even though it sat beside a dilapidated park near the soccer fields, I thought our little tower was beautiful. After all, my daddy had grown up in a small Appalachian house with seven brothers and sisters, brushed his teeth with a branch from a tree, and learned the alphabet in his twenties. So living in Paris felt like a truly cosmopolitan experience.

Then one day the phone rang.

I could tell from my dad's oh-so-casual tone that it was the recruiter for a small Christian college in Nashville. Again. My parents had saved all my life for me to go to this school, which had mandatory curfews and daily chapel, and they arranged for a recruiter to call me every twenty-seven minutes during my senior year in high school. With each phone call, my enthusiasm for the school waned a bit more. One day, instead of passively listening to their I'm-your-best-friend sales pitch, I decided to fight back. I made something up.

"Listen, I want to be a lawyer," I said. "And no decent law school has ever heard of your college."

The recruiter paused for dramatic effect. "My friend David just graduated from here last year and is in his first year at Harvard. Is that decent enough for you?"

Before I hung up the phone, I had agreed to talk to this David about his undergraduate experience at Lipscomb University, which terrified me since I had no real intention of going to law school, nor was I even sure how to spell Harvard. For a week, I read up on the place. And when the phone rang, I was armed with more trivia about the Ivy League than Ken Jennings knows about Norwegian fjords.

"Hello, Nancy. This is David. You're interested in law school?"

When I heard his voice, I knew this conversation was going to change more than my choice of college. He was charming, he was funny, and his idea of a good date didn't involve a cow pasture and two bottles of Michelob. Suddenly, this small-town girl longed for someplace else.

For three years, that disembodied voice on the telephone grew to symbolize that place. One day, walking down a sidewalk in Nashville, I met David face-to-face. He'd moved there after law school and was leaving a client's office when we were formally introduced. Six weeks later we were engaged. Three months later, we were living in Manhattan.

That definitely qualified as someplace else, and I was in for the surprise of my life: evidently not all Americans enjoy Sunday lunch at MawMaw's. This book is the story of the exploration, frustration, and adaptation of a girl taken from Paris, Tennessee, and planted in the middle of the liberal Northeast. It's not an academic tome or an exhaustive investigation into the culture war. Instead, it is just one red American's story about what it's like to live in the blue states, when all she'd ever known was biscuits and church three times a week. Shockingly, I wasn't quite as sophisticated as I'd thought, even though I'd grown up in the shadow of the Eiffel Tower.

So years later when I moved back to the South, did I happily readjust to the slower pace of life and the old-fashioned hospitality?

No. Suddenly, I was irritated at the Wal-Mart cashier talking to a customer about her aunt's arthritis for twenty minutes before ringing me up. Not to mention the serious scarcity of good Vietnamese restaurants.

What had happened to me?

I'd developed a deep appreciation for and frustration with both areas, which was as awkward as being friends with a couple after a divorce. Especially since society constantly categorizes people into different camps (Democrat or Republican, Northern or Southern, Team Aniston or Team Jolie), it's easy to forget both sides have traits we can all enjoy—or at least quirks we can all ridicule. Consider this book a celebration of these cultural idiosyncrasies and enjoy the journey into the dysfunctional family known as America.

Transitions

"Who am I? Why am I here?"
—*Vice Admiral James Stockdale,
in his opening comments as Ross Perot's
running mate in the 1992 vice-presidential debate*

What *Is* a Catfish Queen?

MANY GIRLS DREAM of fairy godmothers, glass slippers, and handsome princes as they drift off to sleep under pink gingham quilts . . . but not the ones in Paris, Tennessee. We liked Cinderella, Sleeping Beauty, and the Little Mermaid, of course, but our favorite princess was no mass-marketed, consumer-oriented creation with figures featured in the latest Happy Meal. Instead, we idolized a princess who never went out of style. Year after year—as we graduated from Slinkys to banana-seat bicycles to training bras to electric-blue eye shadow and shirts inexplicably emblazoned with the Coca-Cola logo—one thing stayed the same. We all dreamed of winning the crown in the Fish Fry pageant, whether we admitted it or not.

I guess that's why I put on a rhinestone necklace and entered the pageant. My dress was actually quite tame compared to the one I'd later wear to the prom, which resembled the grisly aftermath of a run-in between a mermaid and a sequin monster with a glue gun. The dress I'd chosen for the pageant was royal-blue satin, with a straight skirt and a fitted bodice with princess sleeves. I looked nice and slim in it, especially since my permed hair—poufed out to beach ball proportions—created the illusion of height.

I was 5 feet 7½ inches, which my basketball coach rounded up to 5 foot 8 to create a more intimidating roster. Point guard for the Lady Blue Devils that year, I had spent many hours hanging out in our locker room, which smelled slightly of mold and socks. That night, however, it wasn't filled with lanky ballplayers complaining of shin splints. Instead, I walked in my satin shoes (dyed to match my dress) into a war room. Girls and their beauty products were spread out all over the benches, their mothers wielding curling irons with surgeon-like dexterity. A fog of hair spray, permanently depleting the ozone over northwestern Tennessee, engulfed me at the door. People looked up at me in surprise.

"You look pretty," the girls all said, which of course made me feel ridiculous. They were all wearing underwear and T-shirts as their moms worked furiously on their long tresses. When I'd signed up for the pageant, the lady had told me to be there an hour and a half before showtime, which I figured was to make sure no one was late. I had no idea that all the work was done on the premises. "So you'll look fresh," they explained. These girls were pageant experts, having competed in the Fish Fry contests since the Baby Barnyard pageant.

I felt like I'd showed up for the SATs without a pencil. The other contestants, moderately attractive girls I sat behind in math class, looked positively stunning—and they weren't even finished getting ready. Hair was piled high on their heads in large rollers, bobby pins sticking out in every direction like thorns on a rose. Their moms painted makeup on their faces with more care than the Sistine Chapel ever received from Michelangelo. They'd spent weeks attaining the perfect skin tone in the tanning beds so that everyone resembled carrots or incredibly enthusiastic Tennessee Volunteer fans. My skin was as pale as the bar of soap which was, in fact, my only beauty regimen. I didn't know about eyeliner or what "my colors" were, and my lipstick was from the bargain bin at Wal-Mart.

I stood there, shuffling my feet as my freshness left me like a child abandoning a broken toy. As the clock ticked slowly toward seven o'clock, dresses were carefully lowered over Aqua-Netted hairdos. Potbellies were tamed with Lycra, cleavage was created with duct tape, and height was bolstered with three-inch heels.

"Hey, Nancy!" my friend Olivia said. "My rollers are already hot if you want to do your hair." The stunned silence of the room indicated that everyone but Olivia realized my hair was already done. Her mom interrupted with the cheery suggestion, "Let's practice our walks!"

Olivia's mom owned her own beauty shop, sold Mary Kay products, and possessed a huge case of makeup that could magically transform any ugly duckling into a swan, though Olivia was no duckling. Her rich chocolate hair, big brown eyes, and position as head cheerleader made her the most popular girl in the school. Her pink dress was covered in sequins except for the flared bottom that showcased her perfect calves as she sauntered across the locker room with confidence and poise. Wait a minute, I thought. That's *walking*? She looked like a dust bunny being blown gracefully from underneath the bed, and I knew I was in trouble. Just as it never occurred to me to practice my breathing until I took Lamaze classes many years later, I had definitely not practiced walking. I tried a crash course, awkwardly following Olivia across the locker room as the mothers looked away in embarrassment.

"Honey, just stick your boobs out, suck in your stomach, and pretend you've got a book on your head."

As I waited in line behind the curtains of the stage, I was horrified. *Boobs, stomach, book.* Everyone looked better than I did, even the members of the marching band. And they knew how to walk.

When the announcer called my name, I came out onstage and walked from one piece of tape on the floor to the next, forming a triangle of humiliation. "Nancy is the daughter of Bob and Betty, enjoys playing basketball, and likes to hang out with friends." At each piece of tape on the floor, I stopped and smiled at the judges behind a table at the foot of the stage. The announcer ran out of material before I reached the second mark. I mentally kicked myself for not putting more effort into filling out the autobiography paragraph on the application sheet. I could've at least mentioned that I was the school spelling bee champ and enjoyed making fruit baskets for the elderly.

Miraculously, I made it all the way to the second round—beating out the girls who frankly should've stayed home—to the casual-wear portion of the program. Other girls wore polka-dotted sweaters with pleated skirts or matching shorts sets, going for the lunch-at-the-country-club look. My casual ensemble, however, was a striped silk jacket in bold primary colors with gold buttons that, frankly, fit in best under the big top. Although it didn't have a bow tie that squirted water in people's faces, it did have a tie—a long silk one that my dad had to teach me to knot.

It never occurred to me that being prodded onstage like a cow at the state fair was anything less than empowering. I hadn't yet been exposed to a proper women's studies program. A few months later, I'd hear the term "sexual harassment" for the first time in my life, when an incident involving a few girls on the bus and guys with roving hands caused our health teacher to give a stern speech in assembly. (Afterward, the guys joked that they were unaware "harass" was just one word.) Nonetheless, on that night, under the hot lights on the wooden stage, I wanted more than anything to complete my silk-jacket-and-man's-tie ensemble with a fake diamond Fish Fry crown.

After another strut on the stage, we waited nervously in the gym for the top ten to be announced. I could tell by the hooting and hollering that the crowd was getting more excited as the field of competitors was being narrowed. Boyfriends of the participants placed bets on whether their girlfriend would win and sat in the front row like the owners of roosters in a cockfight. The rest of the auditorium was packed, of course, as is always the case—the community attended the pageants as faithfully as the high school football games.

All this goes to show that the Catfish Queen was different from any princess we read about in fairy tales. She wasn't just a pretty face with a hard luck story, rodents turned coachmen, or an inflexible curfew. Rather, she was a carefully chosen symbol of the city of Paris, one with many important responsibilities. Namely, she had the honor of starting the festivities at the Fish Tent by tossing the first hush puppy.

The Fish Tent, of course, was the reason the World's Biggest Fish Fry was in fact so big. In one week, twelve thousand pounds of catfish were fried to golden perfection and served with French fries, white beans, coleslaw, and, of course, hush puppies.

For those of you who aren't familiar with fine Southern cuisine, hush puppies are balls of deep-fried cornmeal usually served with catfish. Mark Twain spoke of them in *Adventures of Huckleberry Finn*, writing, "There ain't nothing in the world so good when it's cooked right." According to tradition, they were so named because Southern Civil War cooks tossed them to their dogs to keep them quiet when Union troops were near, saying, "Hush, puppy!"

People lined up outside the Fish Tent hours in advance to jockey for the first plate of food—guaranteeing not only hot catfish but also a photo in the hometown newspaper, the *Paris Post-Intelligencer*. However, the most important photo of the day was that of the Catfish Queen tossing the first hush puppy to a family member, usually her father, to officially begin the celebration. This tradition became so famous that major-league baseball patterned their season opener after the Fish Fry—but it never was as exciting.

It might seem improbable that the world's biggest anything would occur in Paris, which is well over a hundred miles northwest of Nashville and even further northeast of Memphis. But to me, Paris was America at its best. I had moved to Paris as a child from an even smaller town in Kentucky, so I felt like George Jefferson when he moved on up to the East Side. Paris not only had a Wal-Mart, McDonald's, and Dollar General store, but an

Arby's—a sure sign of civic taste and sophistication. More important, however, Paris had Kentucky Lake—one of the largest man-made lakes in the world, with 2,300 miles of shoreline and year-round boating, hunting, and hiking. But it was the fishing that drew a hundred thousand people every April to our little city of nine thousand residents.

The lowly catfish, a bottom feeder that has the misfortune of tasting good fried, was king that week. Vendors sold Styrofoam fish hats, fish toys, and T-shirts emblazoned with "Paris, Tennessee—Home of Beautiful Catfish and Delicious Women." I felt that particular pride of living in a place that at least some people considered a vacation spot. For absolutely no reason, it made me feel smart. After all, I didn't have to stay at the Best Western to see the catfish races and knew the best location for the premier views of the parade. (Catfish races, by the way, are like any other race, except that they are staged in specially made Plexiglas canals while the townspeople stand around cheering for their specific fish.) I guess the feeling is a little like how sophomores feel upon seeing wide-eyed freshmen walking through the halls holding maps—excited to see fresh faces, invigorated to show them around, and somehow gratified to realize that other people were interested in the place you call home. Many years later, the tourists walking by my apartment near the Liberty Bell would elicit in me the same sensation I felt back then when giving people directions to the Fish Tent.

Paris had a rodeo, several dances, and a carnival that defied all safety and health regulations. Apparently the only job requirement for running the Tilt-A-Whirl was a blood alcohol content above .3 percent, while selling corn dogs simply required an aversion to deodorant. The Catfish Queen made an appearance at each of these events, showing dignitaries around, wearing new outfits, and posing for photos.

In fact, a special section of the *Paris Post-Intelligencer* was dedicated to the winners of the pageants, called "Paris in the Spring." Winners were featured on entire pages with huge photographs and exhaustive biographical sketches. They even posed for advertisements paid for by local businesses, so that they appeared all week in various shots—eating hush puppies at Cindy's Catfish Kitchen, sitting behind the wheel at Carter's Used Cars, and posing with kids on the playground of Miss Betty's Kinder Garden.

"Two, seven, nine, thirteen . . ." As the pageant sponsor read the numbers slowly and sequentially from her perch on the bleachers, contestants and spectators alike crumpled over in tears or jumped out of their heels in joy. I glanced down at the number sixteen written in glitter on a paper plate pinned to my dress and swallowed hard when she jumped from fourteen to twenty-two.

Turns out the only way I could've worn the crown was if I pried it off Olivia's perfectly coiffed head in the parking lot on the way home. I never got to be a Catfish Queen, and Olivia won so many pageants over the years that her dad had to build an addition to the house to showcase her crowns. Our senior year in high school, however, I somehow beat her in our mutual bid for homecoming queen.

Not that a liberated gal like me cares about such things.

My Husband, the Gigolo

WE'D BEEN MARRIED less than a week when the phone rang.

"May I speak to David?" the woman asked in a low, sultry voice.

I hesitated for a moment, handed my husband the receiver, and inconspicuously dusted the coffee table as I eavesdropped on his conversation. This was the fourth time he'd received a phone call from a mysterious woman, and I was beginning to wonder if moving to New York was the best thing for a new marriage.

"Wrong number," he said into the receiver, clicking off the phone and turning his attention back to the Knicks game.

Since David and I married quickly, we didn't have much time for all the preparations of most engaged couples . . . for example, premarital counseling. We were in love, after all, and didn't need advice, even if we'd known each other for less time than it takes for most people to qualify for a mortgage. While some couples make lists of their marital goals and strategies to attain them, David and I made most of our decisions in restaurants around Nashville. When we considered where we should live after our wedding, we could've picked one of our fully furnished apartments in Nashville and consolidated dishcloths. But for some reason when the question was posed, I impulsively said "New York" with as much forethought as a "bless you" after a sneeze.

My only exposure to New York up to this point in life had been through television. *Sesame Street* taught me the city was a friendly place where you could get your toaster fixed, buy a gallon of milk, and learn how to count to eleven all in one square block. Then, *Diff'rent Strokes* showed the Upper East Side embracing Arnold and Willis in spite of their different cultural backgrounds (plus, Janet Jackson was featured in her pre–Super Bowl innocence). George and Weezie "moved on up" and—through capitalistic elbow grease—got a penthouse, a doorman, and a balcony on which George seemed to get trapped during every rainstorm. Later, in *Welcome Back, Kotter*, the Brooklyn students were depicted as wry and edgy folk who managed to exchange lame insults like "up your nose with a rubber hose" in a good-natured but utterly cool way.

It seemed like a tough but appealing city, where people from vastly different perspectives could come and make a go of it . . . the great melting pot that brought together George Jefferson and Mr. Willis, Arnold and Mr. Drummond, Vinnie Barbarino and Washington, and Big Bird and Snuffleupagus. I figured New York would embrace us too.

So, after a careful, deliberative process that took all the way from the lasagna till dessert, we'd decided to move to Manhattan . . . on the condition that our apartment have a view of the Empire State Building—the only building I knew was definitely in New York.

Of course, several people warned me that New York was a decadent place. Dolly Parton once quipped that country people sleep four to a bed because they ain't got no money, but city folk do it because they ain't got no morals. But no matter how many well-meaning people pulled me aside, I shrugged them off.

Mainly because I was bored. I used to sit in the student government offices of my small Christian college and gaze at the photographs of former student leaders. There, to the right of the office door, hung a large group photo of the student officers from 1991, wearing business suits and skirts, lined up in three rows. My eye, of course, always landed on the blond guy in the middle who had called me that day back in high school. I'd never forgotten that conversation; his stories about living in the Northeast fascinated me and made me wish I could be there in Boston with him. Several years later, when I ran into David, I knew exactly who he was. And when we decided to marry, nothing sounded more romantic than escaping to some Northeastern city and creating a life together. New York was honestly the first place that came to mind.

I shrugged off the naysayers, that is, until women started calling the minute we moved into our new postwar second-floor apartment. David kept insisting that they had the wrong number, although wrong numbers don't usually ask for you by name.

When we arrived after our honeymoon in New York's Penn Station with suitcases in tow, the first thing we saw was a fist-fight between a cabbie and a man in a suit. I remember dragging my bags around the altercation and bracing myself for my new life, steeling my resolve to face the daily drama. Had I been visiting, I probably would've turned around and gone home. However, something about being there with David and actually *living* there brought it all down into manageable doses. For example, we didn't gawk at the Chrysler Building, we looked for grocery stores. We didn't stand in line at the Statue of Liberty, we checked out dry cleaners. Plus, since we'd gotten married and honeymooned in France, New Yorkers seemed downright friendly in comparison. After all, we even spoke the same language, mostly.

The most menial chores seemed glamorous and felt significant, just because I was doing them in the City with my new husband. The wallpaper stores were luxurious and posh, my hairstylist name-dropped celebrity clientele, and my mail was delivered from the post office where Newman worked on *Seinfeld*. Even the ATMs spoke Spanish, English, Portuguese, German, Polish, French, or Chinese and required a twenty-dollar minimum withdrawal (no more poor college student five-dollar withdrawals).

In reality, it took me a bit to get used to the close living quarters of millions of people—bustling past one another in the streets, competing for cabs, vying for the last Cherry Coke on the shelf. New York was like my own little *Survivor* set—an exotic location, a limited amount of resources, and everyone fighting for large piles of money. I marveled at how the urban drama played itself out, even in the midst of day-to-day activities. Would anyone hold the elevator door for the guy running through the lobby or would we all pretend not to notice him? Would the bus driver wait for the elderly ladies or make them catch the next bus? Would the pregnant lady on the train be offered a seat or would she have to hang on to the overhead bar?

In the South, I could predict the actions of people with the precision of an actuary. But in New York? I couldn't tell you if the rain there would be wet.

And to compound all the excitement and uncertainty, my husband kept getting calls from strange women. As the calls piled up and as I kept taking messages ("call Cindy," "call Desiree"), I began to wonder if I had been so attracted by all the big-city activity that I'd ignored what was going on in my own marriage. Had I managed to ruin a marriage in less than a month? Most celebrity marriages last longer than that. One afternoon I was reading on the fire escape when it began to sprinkle. Since New York rain, I discovered, was in fact wet, I squeezed myself through our window as the phone began to ring.

"Is David there?" a woman asked. I didn't recognize her voice, but I was beginning to lose track.

When I asked to take a message, the woman paused and said, "Are you lying to me? He's there, isn't he? He told me he could be reached at this number."

This was getting weirder and weirder. "He *gave* you this number?"

"Of course."

"When?"

"Last night."

"Where?"

"At a club in SoHo."

"Are we talking about the same David? Tall, blond—"

"And handsome, of course." Her voice was dripping with sarcasm. "Don't lie and tell me I've got the wrong number."

Although the lady sounded a little unhinged, she was the

first person who didn't nervously hang up when I questioned her. I almost dropped my book when I realized that David hadn't, in fact, gotten home that night until after I was asleep—claiming he had been working late.

"Who are you, anyway?" I guess now it was her turn to ask questions.

"I'm his wife, of course."

"I thought you were his secretary," she said, her voice curt and rude. Then she added, "Well, if it doesn't work out between you, have him call me."

This time it was I who hung up. I realized I had a lot to learn about how people lived in New York. I thought I'd already learned many lessons regarding their lifestyles. For example, they spoke in code. I learned this while apartment hunting. For example, an apartment described as "charming" meant the former occupants painted the walls pink and glued plastic Chihuahuas to the baseboards. "Sunny" meant all the lightbulbs worked. And "spacious" meant you better exhale before entering.

We also learned that quick decision-making skills and money—lots of money—were prerequisites for getting an apartment in Manhattan. David carried the cash equivalent of first and last months' rent in his pocket to make sure we could secure a place we liked on the spot, because if we didn't act immediately, one of the other three million people simultaneously competing for the seventeen available apartments in Manhattan would take it first. We started out early, and our broker took us to ghastly apartments that always seemed to have difficult locks. (We later learned brokers loudly jingle their keys to scare off any cockroaches in the apartment before the clients enter.) He seemed to be under the impression we'd live in an apartment the size of a broom closet as long as it had exposed brick and hardwood floors. Apartment after apartment had close-up views of neighboring building walls and smelled like curdled milk. Exhausted, we almost skipped an interview with the landlord of a Gramercy Park one-bedroom with hardwood floors, a doorman, security system, and a few unique architectural curves. It was "spacious," meaning if you opened the small oven door completely, it hit the other side of the kitchen. And all this for more per month than my parents paid for their five-bedroom, four-thousand-square-foot estate in Tennessee. Most important, though, it had a view of the Empire State Building—if the night was clear and you leaned out the window with your head crooked to the left. Out of a hundred applicants, we were chosen. Evidently our Gap ad looks and Southern manners were bland enough to indicate we wouldn't throw raucous parties.

No, we definitely didn't seem like the kind of people who led wild lives. David was an affable, well-spoken, polite guy. In fact, I had attributed to his natural politeness the fact that he was talking a bit too long to these constant wrong numbers. Once, at three o'clock in the morning, the phone jolted us out of our sleep with its harsh ring. This time, he answered.

"This is David," he said, clearing his throat.

"Sorry, I think you've dialed the wrong number. . . . But I don't *know* a Shannon. . . . You've got the wrong guy."

David at least *seemed* to be exasperated by the calls. He adamantly denied going out to clubs instead of working late but still couldn't figure out the calls. If I left the apartment for just a few hours, I inevitably returned to three or four hang-ups on our machine and one or two messages asking when they could see him again. It just didn't add up.

One afternoon, the phone rang while David was gone, and I was startled to hear a man's voice. "Let me talk to David real quick," he demanded.

"He's at work," I said. "May I take a message?"

"What do you mean, at work? I don't know anything about a job today."

"He works every day."

"Since when?"

"Two weeks ago."

"He's working behind my back?"

"Who are you anyway?" I asked.

"Listen, I've known David for years. The real question is, who are *you*?"

He had a point. I didn't really know anything about the man who was now my husband. I didn't know his friends, I didn't know his hobbies, I just knew one fact. "I'm his wife."

For a moment, I thought the line went dead. "His wife?"

With that, I burst into tears. "We married a couple of weeks ago and strange women have been calling here every hour asking for him. You know him better than I do. What's going on?"

His voice softened. "Everyone knows he's popular with the ladies."

I began to sob even more.

"Do you want me to come over? I'll bring coffee and you can tell me why you guys married so quickly."

"It was a spur-of-the-moment thing," I said.

"Wait a minute. You're not pregnant with a little David Lee, are you?"

"Lee?"

The caller paused. "Well, you can name the kid whatever you like, of course. I'm just surprised David didn't tell me he was going to be a daddy. This might really screw up our comeback."

"I'm not pregnant and my husband's middle name is Austin."

"Listen, I think I know my own client's middle name—it's on all his albums."

Suddenly my sobs were cut short by utter confusion. His agent? Albums? "Are you talking about David *French*, the attorney?"

"No, I'm talking about David *Lee Roth*, the singer."

Now for those of you who spent the 1980s trying to figure out Rubik's Cube, David Lee Roth is the original rock 'n' roll frontman who led Van Halen to worldwide fame. With his long mane of golden hair, acrobatic stage moves, and clothes that put spandex unitards in our collective fashion consciousness, he was the Platonic form of Rock Star—energetic, humorous, and always surrounded by gaggles of women.

On the other hand, my David wore glasses and suits and occasionally cut loose by going to the latest *Star Trek* movie on opening night. In high school and college, he didn't have much time to date because he was busy with his annual reading of the Lord of the Rings trilogy. And his hair, well, what was left of it could not be described as long and flowing. In other words, there had been a colossal mix-up.

The agent and I talked for about half an hour, as we pieced together the facts and realized that David Lee Roth had changed telephone numbers before we moved to the city, yet apparently still gave out his old number to women he met at clubs. For a whole year, when the phone rang, it was most likely a Van Halen groupie. But just in case, I'd pass the phone to my David anyway—there was always the slightest possibility that the woman with the phone-sex-operator voice actually needed legal advice.

This was in 1996, well after Nirvana's "Smells Like Teen Spirit" caused listeners of glam bands to trade in their Lycra jumpsuits for flannel shirts and their perfectly sculpted hairstyles for unwashed coifs. By that time, former Mötley Crüe drummer Tommy Lee had become Pamela Anderson's male concubine, and even I had seen the light and abandoned big hair. It just so happened that, in September 1996, David Lee Roth appeared on the MTV Video Music Awards in New York with Van Halen, fueling rumors that the band was getting back together. During this time span, our phone rang off the hook ("Dude, I just heard the news. . . . Super cool!"), and we got invited to all the good parties in Manhattan. We even talked to his dad.

But women called us day and night. Sometimes they cried in disappointment or asked in defeated tones, "Do many girls call here?" My David, the constitutional attorney, spent much of his free time delicately letting women down on behalf of a rock 'n' roll heartthrob.

If there was a silver lining to this cloud of misunderstanding, it was that we discovered that New York was not filled with people trying to break up our marriage, no matter how decadent its reputation—just brokenhearted women who realized the hard way that David Lee Roth was "Just a Gigolo."

The Birdcage

I KNEW I was no longer at Lipscomb University when a guy stood up and said, "I'd just like to assure everyone I'm a feminist and won't dominate the class just because of my gender." I was sitting in a small room at New York University, and we were going around the room and introducing ourselves with "fun facts." Slow clapping rippled through the room at his proclamation until the ovation reached the level of intensity usually reserved for presidents and Céline Dion. After the applause died down, we learned that Michelle worked for Amnesty International, Cara had been arrested at White House protests six times, and Kim's hobby was shoplifting and destroying foods containing partially hydrogenated oils.

As I racked my brain for fun facts that wouldn't pale in comparison to everyone else's, I braced myself for what promised to be a very different type of educational experience. First of all, the class was called "Philosophy of Sex." Somehow, the same philosophy major that enabled me to study Aristotle and C. S. Lewis at Lipscomb required me to study Catherine MacKinnon and Betty Friedan at NYU. My philosophy classes,

I soon discovered, intersected with the Women's Studies program. For the uninitiated, Women's Studies is the study of why men deserve to be eliminated from the planet just as soon as babies can be grown in petri dishes and pickle jars come with easy-open lids.

Second of all, my fellow class members had very little appreciation of people from the South. When I revealed my name—Nancy Jane—and my fun fact that I had recently gotten married, the students and professor looked at my fresh twenty-one-year-old face and saw the personification of Southern female oppression. It was like they'd just found a piece of tarnished silver in an attic—with a little hard work, I could shine with the freedom that comes with sexual liberation and feminist empowerment, and they started their work right away. They explained that—although I didn't realize it—I was a victim of a male patriarchal society, a heterosexist, and probably a little racist to boot. They told me my Southern culture had imprisoned me in a birdcage of missed opportunities and sexism but that I couldn't see the bars that entrapped me because I'd never known freedom.

All it took to make that assessment was hearing my accent.

This took me aback. After all, I never felt that I quite fit in at my small Southern university, as nice as it was. Nestled in a leafy area of Nashville, the campus was welcoming and regimented, a conservative bastion of female students pursuing their M.R.S. degrees and men wearing polo shirts majoring in business or accounting.

There were also Bible majors, who sat in the front row of the mandatory Bible classes and made the rest of us look lazy for not knowing the Ten Commandments in Hebrew. We all could've been Bible majors after calculating the number of hours we took in these mandatory lessons, with titillating titles like "Acts and the Early Church," "World Religions," and "Old Testament Studies." On top of all the classroom time we spent studying the Bible we also had daily chapel, which was a compact twenty-five-minute church service right before lunch that included a short sermon, songs, and assigned seating.

Because chapel was so short, the sermons were called talks. They were typically as sustentative as Twinkies but left you with an aftertaste of goodwill toward God and your fellow student and ready to face the rest of the day. But there was a more compelling reason to attend—the chapel counter. This was a student chosen for his moral rectitude and mathematical abilities, who stood in the balcony and made sure your seat was filled for the entire twenty-five-minute service. For students whose seats were empty more than ten times per semester, the university took away their scholarship money, suspended their academic privileges, and threw them bound into a giant tub of water to see if they floated.

Chapel was always the same, announcements first, followed by a couple of songs. These weren't hymns like "Rock of Ages" or "How Great Thou Art," which were considered too uncool for the hip college students we were. Instead, we sang catchy, upbeat tunes with words like

If the skies above you are gray, you are feeling so blue . . .

(At which point someone somewhere in the auditorium would invariably echo "so bluuuee," demonstrating a deeper love for

Jesus than the rest of us who sang to camouflage the sound of our stomachs rumbling before lunch.)

If your cares and troubles seem great, all the whole day through . . .

("Day thruuuuuuu . . .")

There's a silver lining that shines, in the heavenly land.
Look by faith and see it, my friend.
Trust in his promises grand!

I liked the singing at chapel most, because something about the talks irked me. It might have had something to do with the fact that only males were able to lead them. I once ran for president of the student government against a guy with two first names, John Michael, with chiseled newscaster looks and a melodic voice. The three-person race narrowed down to a runoff between him and me. One week before the vote, John Michael got up and led a beautiful, spiritually moving chapel talk—providing extra exposure to potential voters that I couldn't attain as a female. After losing solidly against John Michael, I stood up in my 1 Corinthians class and asked, "What about a penis uniquely qualifies a man to lead chapel?"

The other students looked at me in horror as Dr. Black tried his best to placate me with an answer. And so I had become known as the resident liberal at Lipscomb, practically Gloria Steinem, for crying out loud. I expected my transfer to New York University to be like an adopted child meeting his biological parents for the first time and saying, "So *that* explains my nose." I was going to a place full of people who were a lot like me . . .

less rigid in their beliefs, not preaching constantly, and not seeking to validate themselves through men.

However, I soon realized that the students at NYU didn't feel quite the same kinship with their long-lost Southern sibling.

Almost instantly, they honed in on my Christianity. They weren't impressed with my protest against gender inequity at Lipscomb. Instead, they questioned why I had attended chapel at all, challenging my "heterosexist" assertion that God is male and asking me to prove in the Bible that He had male *anatomy* . . . not that they believed the patriarchal Scriptures anyway. (David ran into this as well at Harvard, where the students at the Divinity School were often chastised unless they referred to God as she.)

After mocking my faith, they moved on to the disturbing fact that I wore makeup, shaved my legs, and dyed my hair—my Tennessee bouffant, which I had quickly replaced with a blunt New York cut after I arrived. They said I obviously did all this because I was unwittingly subservient to men. (And they didn't even know about my Catfish Queen attempt, which probably would've prompted a bra bonfire right in the middle of the class.) Countless hours were spent discussing how fashion designers were in cahoots with the American government, as evidenced by the conspiracy to make women sex objects by raising hemlines every time they made advances in the marketplace.

Once we finally stopped talking about how Versace and the White House had shortened miniskirts on the grassy knoll, the talk moved to the lack of affordable day care for working mothers. Since my mom owns a day-care center in Tennessee—Miss

Betty's Kinder Garden brings home first place in the Small Fry Parade contest every year—I had seen firsthand how quality day care, while maintaining the health of the child, is no substitute for a parent's attention. That's all I stated in class, but you would've thought I was trying to replace *Roe v. Wade* with mandatory Epilady treatments.

By the time I was introduced to the theory that all sex is rape, I was beginning to see why my parents lamented my choice of major. For example, we were taught that one in four women has been a victim of rape or attempted rape. To prove her point, my professor asked us to raise a hand if any of us had been raped. When a flurry of hands shot up, I wondered if NYU required emergency room records for admission in addition to good high school grades and a solid SAT score. Then I learned they'd broadened the definition of rape.

For example, we studied Andrea Dworkin, who asserted, "Heterosexual intercourse is the pure, formalized expression of contempt for women's bodies." She also said, "Romance is rape embellished with meaningful looks."

Feminist Catherine MacKinnon said, "Politically, I call it rape whenever a woman has sex and feels violated."

We studied Marilyn French (no relation), who claimed, "All men are rapists and that's all they are."

You can imagine how disillusioned I was to learn that Mr. Rogers, Gandhi, and Bill Clinton were all rapists—well, two of those were shockers. We were also informed that we earned 71 cents on the dollar, suffered massive losses of self-esteem, were ignored by our high school teachers, and were abused on Super Bowl Sunday.

NYU was my bizarro world. While Lipscomb had a dress code, students at NYU thought modesty was an anachronistic practice of sexual repression. The typical image projected by my "Philosophy of Sex" classmates was no makeup, a T-shirt ugly enough to make a statement against the tyranny of fashion but ironic enough to cost $40 in a vintage shop in Greenwich Village, and no bra. I toyed with the idea of passing myself off as a psychic: Let Me Guess Your Political Party—$5! One look at how far down a woman's breasts were hanging and I could tell whether she was a lifelong liberal. After all, gravity does not discriminate on the basis of political orientation, and liberal and conservative women alike should be able to unite on the need for appropriate undergarments.

Other bizarro aspects of my new life involved the interaction between genders. While men at Lipscomb held the door open for ladies, the NYU men let the door smack a woman in the face for fear of being labeled a sexist. The women in my classes considered men to be degenerate and dangerous. Allow me to clarify . . . they considered *heterosexual* men degenerate and dangerous. When the only guy in the back of the class announced he was gay, balloons fell from the rafters, everyone broke into spontaneous applause, and Ed McMahon walked out of the coat closet with a check for a million dollars.

Students there felt free to experiment with the entire concept of sexual identity. Exploration was reinforced with support groups for gays, transvestites, and people questioning their sexuality. There was even a term, "lugs"—"lesbians until graduation"—for women who were temporarily homosexual as a statement of solidarity with their lesbian sisters. And there were

the weaker-willed "bugs"—bisexual women who dabbled in les-
bianism but never could quite give up men. Sexual experimen-
tation was as celebrated at NYU as much as sexual purity was
extolled at Lipscomb. Multiple partners were encouraged as part
of the shopping around necessary for eventual marriage, if anyone was that old-fashioned. The professors and students considered marriage a societal constraint that both limited their sexual
options and robbed them of their identity. Since people in the
North tend to marry and have children much later than their
Southern counterparts, having a family was about as pressing to
them as finding a good set of dentures—something they would
have to look into but not for a very long time.

So, when I announced I was married at the age of twenty-
one, the students collectively gasped. "Does he make you wash
dishes?" "Does he pick up his own underwear?" "Did he make
you take his last name?" In one fell swoop my whole identity as
a free-thinking woman was obliterated, and I wondered if I had
been unfair to the Lipscomb girls who set their sights on marriage from freshman orientation. During my first chapel, the
speaker had said something that almost made me vomit in the
hymnal—that we might be sitting next to our future spouse.
Three years later, as I sat in that classroom in New York, it
slowly dawned on me that I had escaped this marriage-obsessed
environment by . . . getting married. My classmates noticed the
irony.

One thing both places had in common was their ideological
purity—for the right and for the left. Lipscomb professors are not
only all Christians, they are all members of the same denomination. Likewise, upward of probably 90 percent of NYU's faculty

would describe themselves as politically liberal. When they use the word "diversity," they mean some students have dreadlocks, some have red hair, and some are Chinese—the student body version of Rudy Huxtable's friends. The students and faculty looked different but thought identically. I had been so eager to flee the indoctrination at Lipscomb but had no idea NYU would strive to inculcate me with its worldview with much more religious fervor.

This confounded me. In Tennessee, I frequently met Republicans who were conservative but deviated from the Republican party line in some significant personal way. Some were morally opposed to war, others stood against the death penalty, and some even thought Rush Limbaugh was rude. However, the converse wasn't true in Manhattan. I never came across an NYU student who said, "I'm a liberal except I'm opposed to abortion," or "I'm liberal, but that flat tax idea sounds really appealing." I don't even think I met one who wasn't morally aghast at my skeptical attitudes about recycling.

I wanted to be a feminist—the kind that believed in economic equity, human rights for unborn women (and men), and even love. If you have to wash a sock or two, no problem . . . it's the price you pay for the benefit of having feet. But my fellow students would have none of what they called a cafeteria-style feminism. In their eyes, I was a traitor to my gender. In spite of all this, I still wanted to be one of them—just like I wanted highlights and platform shoes. It just seemed so fashionable.

I started believing them when they talked incessantly about the education gap, even though females get better grades and more go to college than males. The Super Bowl–abuse assertion was later proven to be a myth, but the *New York Times* started calling Super Bowl Sunday the "Day of Dread." Also, as Warren Farrell points out in his book *Why Men Earn More*, men gravitate toward higher-paying, more dangerous jobs than women, who prefer safer and more convenient occupations. Neither does the supposed economic gap take into account the length of time in the workplace, age, or experience. I, as a modern American woman who enjoyed more advantages than most women throughout history, began to resent the "glass ceiling."

But of course I didn't recognize the irony. Over the course of many weeks of this kind of teaching, I started wondering if David *was* actually oppressing me—even though he worked seven days a week to pay for a beautiful New York apartment, my private education at a premier university, and a mounting Bloomingdale's bill. After all, we didn't have a dishwasher, I'd known the man for only a few months, and I didn't *like* picking up his smelly socks. In the evenings when he finally dragged himself home from the law firm, I barraged him with questions about the birdcage I was living in. I needed two hours of deprogramming for every hour I spent in class. One semester was all this formerly well-liked Tennessean could stomach, and I packed up my book bag with the accusations of racism and bigotry ringing in my ears.

Suddenly I was a college dropout.

That was in 1996. The Yankees won the World Series, NYU was still tucked in the shadow of the World Trade Center, and the terms "red state" and "blue state" didn't exist. It was a different time, and I was a different person. My education was, in a way, a casualty of the collision between two ideologies. Had I graduated, my life wouldn't be radically different—I'd always want to stay home with my future children. Perhaps with a philosophy degree, I would've encouraged my kids to be the Platonic ideal of Good, spoken to them only in the Socratic method ("Why is wiping your nose on your sister a bad idea?"), and paid a slightly larger student loan bill every month.

It turned out just as well. David was so busy talking to David Lee Roth's ex-girlfriends that we were having trouble fitting in the requisite gender deprogramming every night. However, it did free me up to enjoy Manhattan a bit more—I went to Broadway shows, to television shows (*Regis & Kathie Lee* and, demonstrating a shocking lack of judgment, *Ricki Lake*), and even got a part-time job selling bicycles. However packed my new life of leisure became, one thing remained the same—I always had to wash those dishes.

Six years later, something happened that made my marital birdcage a little less restrictive—David bought me an automatic dishwasher—but I'm still picking up his smelly socks.

This Is Where I Get Off

DAVID ALMOST MISSED my twenty-second birthday. I sat on the edge of my bed in my high-heeled caramel boots as our eight o'clock dinner reservation came and went along with my excitement about my first birthday away from my family. Every year, for as long as I remember, Dad and I had had combined family birthday parties on November 27—sometimes on Thanksgiving, since I was born on the twenty-sixth and he on the twenty-eighth. Daddy always pretended to love the giant princess cake with both our names written in pink icing, and I got one present for every year of my life. Also, I always got one swat on the behind for each year (plus one to grow on) in the curious tradition of commemorating the slap on the bottom doctors give newborns to instigate breathing. But there were no more shared cakes for me. I was having an urban birthday, a married birthday, a sophisticated birthday representing my stylish new life.

During the year we'd lived in Manhattan, I had attended Broadway shows, slipped into afternoon plays, and gotten lost in Central Park with a good book . . . alone. In just a few months, David had metamorphosed from a doting boyfriend into an overworked litigator, and it felt at times that we were still just dating. I'd sometimes go days without seeing him, since he'd come home after I was already asleep and leave for work again before I was awake. He used to spend many hours playing tennis and basketball outdoors when he lived in the South, but his New York existence occurred entirely within the confines of his midtown building overlooking the East River, with helicopters flying beneath his forty-fourth-floor office. Sometimes he'd stay at work for forty-eight consecutive hours, his chair planted firmly against the window (he's afraid of heights), occasionally dozing on his desk till dawn. Then the cycle would start anew.

He worked late so frequently he had more than one secretary—one for day and a team of word processors at night—enabling him to toil away the hours without having to be inconvenienced by the exhaustion of the staff, who apparently had the disadvantage of being mere mortals. Often I brought a change of clothes to his office so he could at least look different from day to day. Once—desperate for some scrap of domestic happiness—I gathered his clothes, made a batch of spaghetti, and caught the midtown bus, hoping for a romantic shared dinner in his tiny office.

At about Twenty-third Street, however, gunshots rang out right in front of the bus, causing the driver to swerve onto a different street. People started yelling—not about the shooting but out of irritation they'd missed their stop on Third Avenue. Terrified into inertia, I didn't get off the bus at the next stop like everyone else. An hour later, the bus and I ended up somewhere near a dark hockey rink outside the city, with a bowl of cold spaghetti nestled in my lap and a wrinkled tie clutched in my sweaty hand. The bus driver took one look at me—the only one left on the bus at the end of his shift—turned the ignition back on, and kindly gave me a private ride to David's office. The Not in Service sign was on as he drove the bus through the streets.

David's demanding schedule had indeed caused some strife in our lives. But I figured he at least could make it to dinner on my birthday. Close to eleven, David called and said he was running late. Trying to salvage what was left of the day, I found a diner still open near our apartment and waited patiently for him to show up.

The waiter brought me a carafe of coffee with two mugs. "Does your husband take cream in his coffee?" he asked, anticipating David's arrival.

We'd been married several months, but the question had me stumped. Later, I discovered David actually takes his coffee one of two ways, depending on his relationship with the person who's offering it. If it's a person close to him, someone he knows well with whom he has a familial, comfortable relationship, he asks for one package of Sweet'n Low and no cream. If it's anyone else, he takes it black, not wanting to inconvenience or embarrass a stranger by asking for a sweetener they might not have available. Southerners are weird that way. Once at a restaurant, my grandmother ate a hamburger without meat—commonly known as a bun—because she didn't want to draw attention to the error of the kitchen staff.

But at that moment, while the waiter impatiently tapped a pen on his notepad, I had no answers. Does he take cream in his coffee? Does he even drink coffee? I didn't know what football teams he liked, I didn't know what he liked to do on lazy Sunday afternoons, and I certainly had no inkling whether he enjoyed cream in his coffee. After all, we barely knew each other when we got married, and he worked so much I hadn't seen him in months.

The waiter glanced at the clock, obviously trying to convey what his desire for a tip wouldn't allow him to verbalize: the diner was about to close and we needed to move this process along. "I guess you don't want to order an entrée for him either, then?"

Minutes later, David lumbered through the front door, pretending to be excited about finding a diner open near our apartment, and handing me a spa gift certificate his secretary had obviously arranged. The new glasses he wore to correct his constant eyestrain didn't hide his tired, bloodshot eyes.

I wondered what we'd gotten ourselves into. My sister Amy had married her boyfriend just a few months before David and I got hitched—probably a financial heart attack to my parents, whose three daughters married in rapid succession. Occasionally I'd hear about Amy's new house in a subdivision near our old college and about the curtains she made to cover the windows looking out onto her small patch of yard. This yard would eventually have a swing set in the back and a small sign in the front that read "Landscape of the Month." She and her husband, Scott, went to church together and attended a weekly Bible study. Their refrigerator was covered with magnets collected from their travels—resin mountains, flags, and birds representing their life together. They traded in their old Honda for a Lexus SUV, which eventually held a couple of baby seats. Their Christmas newsletter was

full of photos—Amy and Scott hiking in the Smokies, Amy and
Scott skiing in West Virginia, Amy and Scott dressed in identical
white shirts on the beach in Florida.

They were a pair; even a casual glance at their refrigerator
showed that. I, however, felt practically single up in New York.
Although David's friends tried to pick up the slack—Damon and
I played racquetball, Jeff hosted a couples Bible study that I attended without David, and Shaunti met me for lunch—it was
still not enough.

One afternoon, David and I sat down for a talk, knee to knee
on our bed. Large dark clouds hung in the sky that day. I imagined hundreds of disappointed tourists waiting in line at the bottom of the Empire State Building, binoculars hanging lazily
around their necks.

"Working this much is going to ruin our marriage," he said.
And my birthdays, I thought.

I tried to remember the details of our short six weeks of dating and wondered how on earth we'd managed to throw together
a wedding during a three-month engagement. My mother was
right. I'd married a rank stranger, less familiar to me now than
he was then.

"I have the perfect solution," I said cheerily, trying to hide
my apprehension. We'd recently gone to California for a wedding, rented a convertible, and drove through the Hollywood
Hills in an unsuccessful quest to touch the HOLLYWOOD sign. It's
a great place, I thought, in spite of the unwelcoming electrical
fence surrounding the famous landmark. The weather's fantastic,
the law firms paid well, and the shopping met the standard to
which I'd grown accustomed. "Los Angeles."

He grimaced like I'd suggested a colonoscopy.

"I was going to suggest Colorado," he mumbled, "so I could work in a ski shop."

Silently I wondered, He skis?

Theoretically, he could have taken a lower-paying job, and we could have moved to Brooklyn or Queens. But then we wouldn't be living in Manhattan—and Manhattan was the entire point. If he had to add a daily commute to his schedule, I might've forgotten what he looked like.

And so we were paying top dollar for an apartment in one of the most expensive real estate markets in America. I was sure if I ever spotted a tree in the city, it would be sprouting money—even my dental assistant wore a gold Cartier watch.

In the South, year-end bonuses are usually gift certificates to local restaurants presented at the holiday party over eggnog, but bonuses in New York can be eye-poppingly large—in fact, we had friends whose bonuses were larger than their whole annual salaries. When they were given out—collectively billions of dollars—new Rolls-Royces paraded their owners around town and dropped them off at their offices, where they were destined to spend another year under the fluorescent light. There was always an incentive to stay just a bit longer, until a certain bonus came through or until a salary increase was given. In this way, life incrementally crept by unnoticed. Although the job was stealing your time, health, and relationships, you always felt you were in control—that you were using the job, instead of the sad reality that it was the other way around.

Once David was in a partner's office when he noticed a picture of a boy in a baseball uniform. "What position does your son play?" he asked. The partner looked at the photograph sitting on his desk as if for the first time before casually answering, "I have no idea."

I'd always thought the Republicans were supposed to be the greedy capitalists, but that was before I moved to the Democratic stronghold of New York. These people were the trendy "latte liberals"—plopping down $7 for a hot drink at Starbucks and feeling morally smug about their "shade-grown," envirofriendly, certified-organic coffee. Eventually, lattes will overrun the red states—probably an instant, chemically heated beverage sold at Sam's Club—but by that time, the blue states will have moved on to the next evolution in drinks, ginseng mint frappuccino, and will look condescendingly at the red states' mass-marketed imitation.

I had no concept of the size of our education loans or how to pay them without David's being handcuffed to his desk. I just knew we were stuck, and a Colorado ski shop was not the answer. It appeared my husband was having a mental breakdown, and I needed to support him.

"Okay," I said, saying the one thing that came to my mind to delay this decision indefinitely. "I think we should pray about it."

Raised in the South, I firmly believed praying might help in a situation like this, when looking in the face of abject poverty and a large gap (financial and geographic) between me and Bloomingdale's. I was sure God would side with me.

One week passed, and we decided not to talk about the decision until we both "heard from God," a phrase David used but whose meaning completely escaped me. During the week, however, I received an answer—or I thought I did. It wasn't an audible voice or a message formed in the sky by cumulus clouds. It wasn't even like hearing a whisper. It was kind of like receiving an e-mail in your head and knowing the contents without having to click on it. Or like a strong impression, a thought that just would not go away no matter how hard I tried to ignore it. So I guess there was a lot of theological wiggle room when I realized I definitely didn't like the answer.

Kentucky.

Immediately, I laughed at my spiritual absurdity. I was no expert at hearing from God, at prayer, or even at making joint marital decisions. Although David had grown up there and his parents still lived there, I had no inclination to go to Kentucky. I'd sent Sally Struthers more than one check to help feed those kids in Appalachia—as far as I was concerned, my spiritual obligation to that state had been satisfied. Comforted by my obvious lack of spiritual maturity, I laughed. Colorado, here we come, I thought, deciding to keep "Kentucky" to myself.

That afternoon, I was already planning what cute ski gear I'd get with David's employee discount. Once I'd taken up tennis just so I could wear a short skirt with bloomers, so I could certainly learn to ski if my jacket was chic. Besides, I'd heard a cold mountain breeze gives your cheeks a healthy glow.

"Kentucky," David said as I settled into my chair, causing me to nearly flip out of it.

"What happened to Colorado? A nine-to-five?" I gasped. "What happened to your thirty percent *employee discount?*"

He breathed a sigh of relief, and the color returned to his face. "Good," he said, obviously relieved. "I must've heard the wrong answer. Can you imagine? Kentucky? There's no good ski-ing in Kentucky."

As he was talking, my breath seeped out of me. Images of our Gramercy Park apartment, Pete's Tavern on Eighteenth Street, and, yes, the Empire State Building sadly faded as he talked. Be-fore I revealed what I had vowed to conceal, I made a pot of cof-fee, figuring the aroma of hazelnut would help our plans seem more palatable. While listening to the coffee drip into the pot, I mentally amended my theological point of certainty to accom-modate a new spiritual understanding—praying might *not* help.

So when I poured the coffee in the mug bearing his law firm's logo, he thanked me and proceeded to drink it black.

Kids

Familiarity breeds contempt—and children.

—*Mark Twain*

Casserole, Good for the Soul

BECAUSE SOUTHERNERS TEND to spend so much time under the steeple, no phase of life can pass by without the church being right there helping you, like a well-intentioned mother-in-law. Premarital counseling, divorce recovery, weight loss classes, addiction therapy, and visits to shut-ins are routinely offered to congregants in need. In the case of a loved one's demise, the church activates with a flurry of activity—the men start praying, the ladies start their Crock-Pots, and friends head straight over to sit with the bereaved. Since the church views death as a homecoming, sadness is usually tinged with humor, and the best food can always be found at the home of the deceased. I've heard of people stopping by for the banana pudding like others crash weddings for the cocktails.

The only other occasion that merits as much activity in the church as a death is a birth. I found this out when I became pregnant in Georgetown, Kentucky. Now bear in mind, I didn't feel ready to have a baby. In fact, just months before, we'd decided we weren't ready to be parents and embarked on activities available only to the childless and carefree.

First, I bought the tiniest electric-blue bikini I could and still, in good conscience, call myself a Christian. Second, we took a seven-day Caribbean vacation that I jokingly referred to as the I-don't-have-stretch-marks cruise. Then we drove right past a car lot of minivans, and proceeded to buy a fire-engine-red Jeep Wrangler—no carpet, no air-conditioning, and, most tellingly, no backseat.

David installed a mount on the top and operated it as a tank during his paintball battles, and all my clothes ended up smeared with the dye that inevitably ended up on the seats. Paintball, a sport that makes otherwise normal people channel Rambo and communicate in monosyllabic grunts, is a more dangerous version of laser tag. So many guys at our church played it that the church secretary got a call from someone asking, "Who's in charge of your paintball ministry?" She referred him to David, because he was the oldest person in the whole league—the Billy Graham of paintball.

One day David was cleaning his new paintball gun in the living room of our Victorian home in Georgetown, Kentucky, when I saw him aim his weapon at the cooler.

"What'd that cooler ever do to you?" I asked.

He waved his hand in front of my face, and after he uttered some dubious mathematical calculation involving the speed of the balls, the proposed range, and the assertion that the one-inch-thick Styrofoam would stop anything less than a speeding train, he pointed his gun and pulled the trigger. David always used pink paint, to further humiliate his victims, and in one quick second I comprehended the color's acrid offense. As I sat on the comfortable cushions of the first sofa I'd been able to afford—a Shabby Chic knockoff, without slipcovers to save money—I watched my apartment become an instant war zone. It looked like an acid reflux patient had chugged a whole gallon of Pepto-Bismol and promptly gotten sick in my living room— from the ceiling to the walls, the lamps to the computer.

When I found out I was pregnant, David jumped up and down on the newly pink polka-dotted cushions of my couch holding the pregnancy test with the faint blue lines. I didn't know it, but in a few short months, that same sofa would sport breast-milk stains, Crayola smudges, and an Oregon-shaped Kool-Aid blob.

The ladies in the church activated and threw me a baby shower that would've outfitted triplets, which is exactly what they accused me of having once I ballooned up to my two-hundred-pound glory. (By the last trimester, posing naked in *Playboy* would've made me less insecure about my body than attending Sunday school and hearing, "You look like you're about to burst!" several times before the opening prayer.)

Showers traditionally occur before weddings and births, and in church they're usually held in multipurpose rooms or gymnasiums decorated in pink or blue gingham. All the church women, even the ones you don't know, come dressed in their finest. They always bring food—usually something congealed, the color of seventies appliances, and brimming with marshmallows and unidentifiable fruit—that is placed on the long, plastic-covered tables lining the wall. By the time everyone has shown up, the table is filled with miniature hot dogs, nuts, sausage balls with toothpicks, and, of course, a cake. For some reason, the grocery store cake is how Southern churches commemorate all life's special occasions—maybe since alcohol is often prohibited—and the cursive icing congratulates newlyweds, welcomes babies, honors promotions, and celebrates retirements. You can always tell who's a good Christian by whether she grabs the first corner piece with the icing roses or if she dutifully passes it along.

The ladies also come with gift bags—large ones printed with Scriptures in calligraphy and overflowing with tissue paper. As I opened each one, I tried not to smile at the little tags addressed to "Nicki" or "Amy," which the givers had obviously forgotten to remove before recycling the bags. In fact, only about forty bags have ever been purchased collectively by the people at Trinity Church, but they've been kept in constant circulation since the Reagan administration.

By the time I left the church gymnasium, I had more blankets, pacifiers, and diapers than I knew what to do with. In fact, I didn't know what to do with any of it . . . but I never lacked advice.

"Start reading the Bible to that child right now," one lady said. "It's never too early."

"Do you really think you should eat those M&M's?" another asked.

And whenever I'd reveal name options, they'd wrinkle up their noses, put an arm around my shoulder, and helpfully run through all variations of playground nicknames possibly derived from them. They were so creative in their mutations that I began wondering if these upstanding church folk had been school bullies themselves before walking the straight and narrow. Eventually I decided on the name Camille, ignoring their warnings that mean-spirited kids might call her the Chameleon. But none of them predicted my sister would call her Camilli Vanilli (after the lip-synching lotharios) or that she'd later call herself Happy Mille (after her favorite McDonald's entrée).

Yes, the people at church provided everything I could've needed. The pastor's wife was a nurse who gave me breast-feeding advice, the elderly women offered babysitting services, and a teenage girl from the youth group came over to my house with an Arby's bag after I complained about feeling too tired to cook.

However, a couple of emotional outbursts almost ruined it all. The first happened on a Friday night, when the "ministers of paintball" planned a battle that was supposed to conclude at midnight on a nearby farm. The girlfriends of the guys (few were married, since David tended to participate in activities that only teenage boys found enjoyable) came over to our little house, sat on our stained sofa, and ate a pizza while we waited for the boys to come back, bragging about their war wounds. Midnight came and went, as did the hours of one, two, three, and four o'clock. When David finally appeared at five, I was delirious with hormone-enhanced rage. He'd just been bragging about what a cool wife I was to his buddies when he came through the door and received a furious tongue-lashing that paralyzed everyone with fear. By the time I was done yelling I was shocked to see that they'd somehow managed to slip out the door unnoticed.

The next week, David and I went out to dinner with a young married couple right after my doctor had told me to avoid sugar until the next appointment. We sat in Cracker Barrel, looking over the menu, when my eyes landed on my favorite meal,

Momma's Pancake Breakfast. I could smell the pancakes and imagine the thick syrup running down the sides and over the sausage. When David gently reminded me of the doctor's orders, I almost burst into tears. The waitress asked, "Honey, are you having a bad day?" I quickly responded, "No, I'm just having a bad *marriage.*" We ate in silence, and no one dared to order pancakes.

I'd managed in one short pregnancy to offend just about everyone in the church. In fact, the night I went into labor, I skipped the Sunday night service—too embarrassed by my behavior to face people—and began cleaning out my refrigerator. When I felt that unmistakable pain in my back, my first and most pressing thought was that I must shave my legs, since of course this was the day I hadn't. Or, rather, the month. I ignored David's protests and got into the shower until the pain became too much to bear, and we sped down I-75—my head dripping wet from the shower and my fat legs as smooth as apples.

When I finally made it to the maternity ward at Central Baptist, my debilitating contractions made it difficult to concentrate on the nurse's inane questions. "Address?" "Birthday?" I was stretched out on a hospital bed by the third question, being wheeled to the delivery room as she made notes on a clipboard. "Weight?" Instinctively I answered, "One hundred and sixteen pounds," a patently false prepregnancy weight I'd given out since I'd gotten my Tennessee driver's license at age sixteen. The nurse took one look at my bursting stomach and swollen face and said, "Sugar, you may've weighed one sixteen at some point in life, but you sure don't tonight."

The Scriptures, spelled out in brass letters on the corridor walls leading to the delivery room, comforted me ("Behold, children are a gift from the Lord"), but I was ecstatic when the anesthesiologist walked through the door. As that sweet medicine surged through my veins, I vowed to get an epidural with the next kid, even if we adopted. For most of my active labor, I was in a deep sleep while David watched an NBA basketball game. But when the doctor told me it was time to start pushing, David immediately metamorphosed into a sensitive, caring birth coach. "You better push now or this baby's gonna have a cone head!"

As soon as nine-pound Camille was measured, poked, prodded, and bathed, the obstetrician asked us if he could lay hands on the baby for prayer. He assured me this was his custom, and not because Camille's vigorous screaming made him figure we'd need all the help we could get.

The tradition of laying on of hands is based on the Judaic practice of conferring blessings and authority to people. Jesus laid hands on the sick while healing them and on young children when he blessed them. Televangelists have appropriated the practice to make the work of the Holy Spirit look like a knockout Mike Tyson might use in the ring, but this doctor was gentle when he laid his palm on Camille's head. I don't quite remember what he said. The nurses were working quietly, Camille was shrieking, and David looked terrified at the new bundle of responsibility. I just remember when he said amen, I succumbed to the tranquilizing effect of the drugs and exhaustion.

The next morning, the nurse awoke me to tell me I had visitors waiting. Apparently the church had reconvened in my hospital room, after stopping in early the previous night. Literally dozens of visitors stopped by to see the baby—people whom I knew and cherished and their closest friends, relatives, coworkers, and acquaintances. They filled my hospital room with flowers and balloons, and the church bulletin announced the following week I'd delivered a nine-pound whopper. (The women who'd warned me about my diet probably exchanged knowing glances.)

I didn't take to motherhood naturally. For some reason, I couldn't change diapers, breast-feed, and brush my teeth all in the same twenty-four hours. Sensing my panic, people from the church showed up at our house every night with food—I always knew it was six o'clock when one of countless women knocked on the door with a white Corning Ware dish with her name written on the bottom in permanent marker. She'd smooth my hair, rock the baby, and listen as I complained about my lack of sleep. Aided by these innumerable casseroles, David and I slowly acclimated to parenthood. In fact, I came to realize that all the biblical passages about healing and love were best encapsulated by the instructions "Bake it for thirty minutes at 350 degrees" and "You'll know it's done when it's crispy on top."

Nipple Confusion

SIX MONTHS AFTER Camille was born into the land of church and casseroles, David got an opportunity to teach at Cornell Law School in upstate New York. Reluctantly we left the warm embrace of our church friends and headed up the interstate, where the annual snowfall is seventy inches and the average number of sunny days per year is eleven. Cornell sits on a hill in Ithaca and overlooks Cayuga Lake, the largest of the Finger Lakes, which is forty miles long, four hundred feet deep, and so cold that I never got more than a toe wet. The college is surrounded by deep gorges, rolling hills, rich farmland, and Riesling vineyards. When we saw the gorgeous architecture of the buildings in photographs, my mind raced with thoughts of a small, quiet life punctuated by weekend trips to New York City.

When we arrived, however, we noticed that this was a town like none we'd ever experienced. On our first visit to the doctor, the pediatrician told us that the town's water supply was not fluoridated and prescribed little drops for me to administer daily to Camille. "But be careful," he said. "She might get cavities if you give her too little, but her teeth will discolor if you give her too much." I got a little anxious. "Why don't they just put fluoride in the drinking supply?" I asked. The doctor smiled at my ignorance. "Ithacans don't trust the government to medicate them."

Soon afterward, I learned many Ithacans don't even trust *doctors* to medicate them. When I got pregnant with my second child, I found myself in several conversations with people about childbirth and labor. Some hired midwives for birthing at home, some gave birth in the hospital in underwater tanks, and some used hypnosis. Pretty unanimously, however, they were against pain medication.

I tried not to recoil as they explained their reasoning: natural birthing gives you more control of your body, a sense of female empowerment, a better bond with the baby, and even—some claimed—the best orgasm of your life.

"Excuse me?" I asked, figuring they were kidding the girl from the small town.

But they were serious.

In other words, these mothers did things a little differently from the mothers I knew in Kentucky. They wore their infants in slings, were adamant about the benefits of co-sleeping, and made their own baby food.

I wanted a basic no-frills labor (as well as someone to sue in case of complications), so I went to the only hospital in the region. Even there, however, I couldn't replicate my relatively easy and (what I considered) traditional birthing experience in Kentucky. During one of my first checkups, they told me they didn't administer epidurals—which made me suspect there was something funny about the water in Ithaca other than its lack of fluo-

ride. Although they offered other ways to manage the pain, I received this news with as much enthusiasm as if I were about to
experience a root canal without Novocain or a Michael Moore
film without earplugs.

A few weeks before the baby was due, David and I went in
for my weekly checkup at the doctor. Since the appointment was
early in the morning, I dropped Camille off at a friend's house—
still in her pajamas—planning on picking her up before lunch.
However, my doctor suspected that I'd lost amniotic fluid over
the weekend. "I think you should go straight to the hospital," he
said. "We're going to have to induce."

This was not the deliriously joyful sprint-into-the-shower
excitement we'd had previously. We drove solemnly to the hospital, listening to upbeat CDs as I dabbed the corners of my eyes
with a tissue. When we got to the delivery room, we noticed a
poster on the wall which read, inexplicably, "Some People Say
Babies Are Made in Heaven, but We Know Better." During my
contractions, David and I debated whether this was some sort of
feminist statement or a vile sexual joke, an issue never fully resolved since doctors and nurses kept coming in to get free tuto-
rials from David on Florida election law. I guess I forgot to
mention I went into labor at the height of the 2000 Bush-Gore
election drama, during which David had taken it upon himself
to become an expert on the conflict. He even divided his Cornell class into two opposing sides and graded them on how well
they defended their candidate. (He had to assign some of the liberal Cornell students to the Bush team, of course, since few
wanted to associate with that side.)

"Remember me?" I felt like screaming as the contractions

grew more intense. But no one did. For a month, most Americans did little else but discuss the possible outcome of the election. I remember the doctor asking David who he thought was going to win, which transformed our delivery room into a makeshift poli-sci class, as several nurses and hospital staff members came in to hear David's professional opinion.

I gave birth to a wonderful baby boy that December day, minutes after the Supreme Court decided on a technical argument to give Bush the victory by the narrowest of margins. My husband and I were thrilled on both counts.

But political euphoria can last only so long. The nurses dampened the mood when they brought in a stack of white cloths and plopped them on the counter. "Do you know how to use these?"

"What *are* those?" I asked.

Apparently, I was told, this hospital was environment-friendly—and since cloth diapers don't sit in a landfill for two million years, our baby was fated to urinate down his leg. Before I could argue that using leaky anachronistic diapers was unfriendly to *my* immediate environment, I noticed my son wasn't nursing.

Now, you must realize this hospital encouraged breast-feeding with as much fervor as airports "encourage" passengers to leave their firearms at home. In addition to outlawing Pampers, it outlawed all bottles or pacifiers that could potentially cause so-called nipple confusion, which prevents babies from latching on during breast-feeding. In other words, everyone was disturbed when my newborn wasn't nursing properly. Alarms sounded, lactation consultants rappelled from the rafters, and therapists reserved time on their calendars to heal my son's wounds from his broken postnatal bonding experience.

We soon discovered, however, he was having trouble nursing because he was having trouble *breathing*. Evidently, the doctors had calculated his due date incorrectly, an error that had gone undetected because of their reluctance to do ultrasounds. When he was born, he looked premature and the doctor commented that he didn't look quite ready for the world. But since he had scored well on his Apgar test, we were all surprised when his lung collapsed; he had pneumonia. For days, he was encased in a plastic bubble in the neonatal intensive care unit. Going to great lengths to ensure he didn't experience an unnatural feeding, the nurses nourished him by injecting milk into a nasal tube leading to his stomach. Not only could I not breast-feed him, I couldn't even hold him.

Realizing I wasn't able to comfort my new son—who was crying when he wasn't panting for air—I broke down and asked for what is perfectly acceptable in the South but considered gauche in Ithaca: a pacifier. The nurse refused this basic comfort, explaining the baby could be confused by foreign nipples. No pacifiers were allowed in the hospital. Frustrated by her draconian adherence to these peculiar rules, my husband slammed his fist down. "In our family, we don't believe in nipple confusion. We practice nipple diversity!"

She was not amused. And neither were we, frankly. The fact that I'd never been separated from Camille complicated matters infinitely. In fact, she was still at the house of my friend, who had graciously agreed to extend her babysitting responsibilities beyond breakfast . . . into three days. And we weren't even *that* close. Not to mention Camille had nothing except the footed pajamas she was wearing. Eventually David's parents made the drive up from Kentucky and relieved my friend while our son battled for his very breath.

For ten days, we waited in the intensive care unit and spent the late nights alone with the nurses in the neonatal unit. As the hours passed, we cajoled them into telling us the weirdest things they'd ever seen while working in Ithaca. When they started talking, the anti-Pampers, antipacifier hospital staff suddenly looked like Pat Buchanan compared with their leftist, hippie patients.

A nurse named Lucy told us of several patients over the past twenty years who had brought placenta recipes to the hospital, so the parents could eat the placenta one to three days after the birth. Ostensibly, this replaces vitamins and minerals lost during the birthing process and enables both parents to connect with the "spirit" of their child more quickly. Roasting was the most common method, but some people dehydrated the placentas for consumption later.

"Like placenta jerky?" David asked. For some patients, this was the only meat they'd ever eat, since it was gained through a nonviolent act. (Although I think giving birth without an epidural might either qualify as a violent act or prompt the mother to commit one against the anesthesiologist.) The number one justification of this behavior: since animals eat their placentas, it must be quite natural. After the nurse explained this, David mumbled, "Dogs eat their own excrement too."

"Speaking of animalistic behavior," Lucy went on, "we once had a father who wouldn't let us bathe his newborn son after he came out of the birth canal."

"Why?" David asked.

"He wanted to *lick* the mucus off the child."

As David almost fell off his chair, she continued, "And once a group of friends came into the delivery room when this lady was in heavy labor. They burned incense, dimmed the lights, made a line, and fondled each other—including the laboring woman."

"Wait, wait, wait," David demanded, "like some sort of sexual conga line?"

"I don't know, but periodically, someone would yell, 'Switch!' and the person in the front would go to the back of the line, changing partners. Eventually I told them burning incense was not allowed in the hospital and it evidently broke the mood."

"Well, finally, this hospital was forbidding something for a legitimate reason."

"To top it all off"—she leaned in conspiratorially—"the lady's husband even stimulated lactation by *nursing* her during her contractions. In front of everyone."

One day slowly relented into the next, with us passing our time in late-night conversations with nurses about the crazy election and hippie birthing rituals. Over the course of our stay, our persistent pacifier pleadings wore down the nurses' resolve. Eventually we bought a pacifier for ten dollars on the black market—from Lucy, who kept a stash in her purse. And even better, she gave us a special dispensation of Huggies after the cloth diapers failed to adequately protect their expensive medical equipment. Approximately two days later (on Camille's second birthday), we left the hospital with a healthy baby boy.

Now, that couldn't have been a coincidence.

Attack of the Androgenoids

WHEN DAVID RECEIVED an opportunity to teach at Cornell Law School, I happily envisioned a quaint college town, ivy-draped buildings, and meaningful conversations with the intelligentsia. But when we arrived, I suddenly felt embarrassed about being a college dropout. David assured me it didn't matter (he always bragged to people, "My first wife *is* my trophy wife"), but the Ivy League environment constantly reminded me of my academic shortcomings. While I attended functions at Cornell, dined with professors, and went to my Bible study with four biochemistry Ph.D.s, I felt dumb. Not only were the other mothers in my group successful academics, they talked about their disciplines in their free time. If I heard one conversation about punctuated equilibrium, I'd heard a dozen. After a few months of academic talk, I began to wonder why I got along so well with David—no academic slouch—but fell into a coma of boredom while talking to the average Ithacan.

"I'm an intellectual by profession, not for entertainment," he explained, cleaning his paintball gun as he watched *The Terminator*.

Nonetheless I had a pleasant group of friends who met for playgroup every week, and I trudged out onto the frozen tundra with my two-year-old and infant hoping against hope they wouldn't catch the pneumonia going around. In the South, people catch colds. But in Ithaca, it was always dire—pneumonia, foot-and-mouth disease, scurvy. It didn't help that everyone was lackadaisical in their sippy cup patrol, feeling that sharing drinking cups promoted communitarianism. Afraid of looking like a greedy capitalist obsessed with quaint notions of private property, I'd watch as a kid would grab Camille's drink and proceed to smear his snot all over it. "It's fine," I'd say before tossing it in the garbage.

Sometimes we'd sit around discussing breast-feeding in hushed, reverential tones, suckling children young and old. I always had a kid attached to me as well—when the doctor cut the umbilical cord, my baby had just permanently reattached at the nipple. So in some regards I fit in quite nicely there and enjoyed breast-feeding's lack of stigma in Ithaca—women nursed at the park, at dinner parties, in grocery stores, and even at church. But when I began to wean Austin after fifteen months, I encountered some unexpected contempt.

"Why are you depriving him of mother's milk so early?"

"Are you feeling pressure by society to wean?"

"Is your husband making you do this for sexual reasons?"

The fact I'd been lactating or pregnant for most of Clinton's second presidential term didn't impress these people. It was common in that town to see offspring walk up, yank their mothers' shirts up to nurse, and run off to read Dostoyevsky. And when my pediatrician told me of a woman who simultaneously breast-fed all three of her children—an infant, a three-year-old, and a five-year-old—I tried not to wince.

But women who breast-fed excessively were not questioned. Rather, the targets of constant criticism were average mothers who struggled with the demands of leaky breasts, diet restrictions, and sleepless nights (and were relieved to give it up after "only" fifteen months).

I always felt sorry for one poor mother in our group who couldn't lactate and had to defend her medical condition to newcomers every week. Her doctor's name was mentioned with knowing smirks and the kind of disdain a teacher would have for the school-yard drug lord. Enfamil, cocaine—both represented extreme moral failure.

About eleven days a year, it was warm enough to take our playgroups to the city park. One day I was basking in the rare glow of the warm sun (I typically got as much exposure to the sunlight as the most conservative burka-wearing Muslim) when suddenly I noticed a little tyke wearing a football jersey run right in front of Camille's swing. Panicked, I lunged, jerking the black rubber swing abruptly. The child's frantic mother ran up to thank me for averting disaster. "No problem," I said. Then, making small talk as moms do in parks, I asked, "How old is your son?" The lady looked at me with no trace of irony and said, "His name is Jill, and she's three."

As my mind was trying to sort the pronouns and antecedents, she went on to explain she belonged to a group of parents who rebelled against gender stereotypes, choosing to allow their children to decide for themselves which gender they preferred after they'd been exposed to both options. I was well acquainted with this line of thought from my days at NYU: children are born with sex but taught gender and unwittingly learn certain gender signifiers that dictate their behavior. In other words, they believe little boys don't naturally want to play with trucks and little girls aren't naturally drawn to dolls if left alone by eager parents who try to indoctrinate children with heterosexist ideas about gender. Gender roles, they claim, cause people to live according to the very limited ideas of others. The ultimate goal, of course, is androgyny, where no differences between males and females exist.

"I'm going to raise her as gender-neutrally as possible and let him decide which gender she prefers at the age of eight."

Oh, eight—I thought. That magical age, when everything in the world is clear and you're able to start making the decisions that will determine the rest of your life. I wondered if this little kid was actually a boy or a girl and whether the kid even knew. I'd heard of little boys being sent to kindergarten in dresses in Ithaca, but I'd never met one of the parents I mentally referred to as androgenoids. In Ithaca, people just smile and encourage these unfortunate kids as best they know how. In the South, this parent would have been arrested.

To be fair, Ithaca is the most extremely blue area I've seen. It elected a socialist mayor, cast more votes for Ralph Nader than George Bush in the 2000 election, and had a female police chief whose two biggest accomplishments were going topless in public to promote equal rights for women and banning the American flag on police uniforms. So it's not fair to equate Ithaca with more reasonable blue areas. However, it is safe to say there are legitimate differences in the way parents in the red states and people in the blue states raise their children.

Many years later, I sat with a different group of mothers in Philadelphia talking about how their boys liked manicures and wore clothing from the fashion district in New York.

"Oh, I just let him get a little polish while I'm getting my manicure," a couple of mothers explained to a group, who nodded in agreement, as if kindergarten nail care was a must-have skill for boys. Quickly I tried to remember the last time I had even trimmed Austin's nails and scanned the playground, hoping I wouldn't see him accidentally shredding a playmate's face with his neglected, ungroomed fingernails.

What I saw was even worse. My kid was playing Power Rangers—anathema to the ladies sitting at the park—and was teaching all the other little boys how to fight the evil Lothor.

"Stop!" I almost yelled. "They'll break a nail!"

But I didn't have to intervene. Several of the other mothers had already noticed what was going on and were immediately on the scene.

"We don't play *Power Rangers*," one of the mothers said, saying the words with the kind of expression most people would reserve for "diarrhea" or "lumpy vomit." The mothers shared an appropriately sober look, silently wondering whose bad parenting was to blame. Luckily, the immediate suspect was my friend Rene, whose son had dressed up as the red Power Ranger for Halloween. Sensing all eyes were on her, she went on to describe the cutest costume she had seen—a youngster dressed up as the Dalai Lama.

I marveled at Rene's ability to fit into almost any group, listening to her rave about the simplicity of the costume—comprised of a robe and a look of holiness—because I hadn't yet come out of the closet with my Philadelphia friends. They didn't know I was a Republican and therefore actually preferred a high violence quotient in my children's television programming. As they talked, I vowed to remain closeted for as long as possible.

Over the course of our friendship, parenting differences became laughably apparent. Once, when I left my kids at the park in the hands of some other parents, Camille became inconsolable over a boo-boo. Several of the parents gathered around her and discussed how to comfort her in my absence. Rene offered, "Nancy usually says something really eloquent about Jesus or the Bible or something."

Elena, an atheist, stepped up to the plate. She patted Camille on the head and said stiffly, "Be happy, God will . . . heal you." Seeing that didn't work, Rene—who's quite agnostic—talked to her about the importance of prayer. Finally my friend Jack, an Orthodox Jew, talked about Adam and Eve and how God had taken care of them by making them clothes, which somehow held her over until I returned. I was touched they even tried.

I had much less success in the reverse situation, when I watched Rene's sons Ethan and Jack at the park one afternoon while she dashed to a nearby store to get lunch. Of course, as soon as she left, Ethan hurled a Hot Wheels car through the air and hit Austin in the head. He obviously didn't mean to hit Austin. But when I saw the car flying through the air and let out a gasp, Ethan was so embarrassed he ran off to the other side of the park. Spread out like that, it was nearly impossible for me to keep an eye on all four kids at once . . . and Philly parks are always a mixed bag of happy yuppie couples and drug addicts under the slide. But no matter what I did, I couldn't coax Ethan out from behind the tree. I tried kindness, I tried apologizing, I tried bribes. Eventually, I said, "Ethan, just obey me, please!"

It was the wrong thing to say. He planted his feet firmly in the dirt, hugged that tree, and wouldn't have moved even if the Power Rangers themselves had shown up and asked. By the time Rene returned with lunch, I was flummoxed. Ethan was near tears, and the other kids were doing somersaults off the monkey bars. When I told Rene the story, she smiled knowingly. "We don't use the word 'obey' in our family," she explained, saying he probably didn't even know what it meant. "It sounds too . . . biblical. We prefer to use words that are less judgmental."

And I had a lot more to learn. One day I was drinking coffee at my friend's house when our friend Meredith showed up with exciting news.

"I think Zoe is an indigo child!" she said, grinning from ear to ear. "Both her pediatrician and teacher think so."

Meredith is an attractive mother of two, whose husband takes the train to New York every day to his lucrative job. She possesses a quick sardonic wit, incisive intelligence, and a playful manner that makes her fun to be around. Her older child Zoe is as delicate as a doll, with chestnut ringlets and boundless energy.

"Her doctor told me about a new type of child being born after 1992," she continued, "who behave differently than ever before in history. Well, sociologists have never seen so many at once. Like, have you noticed how so many children are being medicated these days?"

I agreed. Many of the kids in my mother's kindergarten were

more strung out on Ritalin than my friends at NYU were on co-caine.

"It's because teachers don't know how to handle these new types of children," she said. "Humans have evolved to the point where almost eighty-five percent of children born after 1992 are indigo children. And don't tune me out because I said the word 'evolved,' I know that drives you Christians nuts."

"Keep going," I said, still very confused. "What does the color have to do with it?"

"You know, indigo, like their life color."

I looked at her blankly.

"Her *aura*," she said. "Don't tell me you haven't had your aura read."

"Not so much."

"Like, have you ever noticed how old paintings of Christ have large circles drawn around his head?"

"Yes!" We were finally communicating. "A halo?"

"That's a common misconception. Those are some of the first artistic depictions of auras in history." I watched Zoe, who'd been yelling "I'm a beautiful indigo child" for the past half hour, climb onto a half wall dividing the kitchen and the living room. Her feet barely fit on the narrow ledge, and she thrust out her hands with the showmanship of a tightrope walker at the circus. "It's scientifically proven. Haven't you read about the vibrations all living things emit? It all takes place on a subatomic level and has to do with electrons and protons. You probably don't believe in science because of your beliefs about creationism, right?"

I ignored her in an effort to truly understand what she was getting at. "Who exactly reads auras?"

"Psychics, mediums, spiritualists." She glanced over at her indigo daughter as she now balanced herself precariously over several simmering pots on the stove. "Be careful, Zoe."

"So," I said, trying to narrow our conversation to one whacked-out idea at a time, "these indigo children all have the same color aura?"

"Exactly!"

"And how do you tell your child is an indigo child?"

"There's a test," she said as she unfolded a crumpled piece of paper her kid's teacher had given her. "If you answer yes to several of these questions, you probably have an indigo child. I'm sure Camille's one." She cleared her throat. " 'Does your child act like royalty and have difficulty with discipline and authority? Does your child refuse to obey?' "

Meredith motioned for Zoe to get off the wall. " 'Is waiting in lines torture for your child?' " She looked at me in astonishment. "You should've seen Zoe at Disneyland. 'Is your child a *nonconformist?*' "

I eyed Zoe nervously as she tottered on the wall between a large leather chair and a pot of water we were heating for spaghetti.

" 'Does your child refuse to respond to guilt trips, get bored easily, and display intuition? Is she very intelligent and does she daydream a lot? Does your child have unusually large eyes?' "

Meredith placed the pasta in the pot. "She's got eyes like dinner plates. Get down, Zoe—you'll fall and get burned!"

We talked about this for hours, as Zoe jumped on and off the wall, giggling, bouncing, and exclaiming, "I'm an indigo child!" Perhaps over all the yelling, I hadn't heard Meredith correctly, I thought. So, when I got home I did a little research about the phenomenon. "Indigo children" apparently go by different names, like "children of the sun" or "the millennium children," and psychics debate why they are making their appearance at this point in history. Some claim aliens have been abducting and manipulating the DNA of these children to prepare the rest of us for the eventual unveiling of the alien life-forms on earth. Some think the children are themselves aliens. Most, however, think these children are reincarnated geniuses preparing to teach us great spiritual truths, which explains why they are hesitant to obey their parents and are unruly in school. After all, if you were Cézanne in a previous life, how could you be content doing color by numbers?

The more I read, the more my heart sank. I found out a psychic in Reno, Nevada, had channeled much of the information about these children from a god named Kyron. Kyron is described as "one who has been here from the beginning." Sidelined for centuries by a hateful world, Kyron has apparently eked out a living by writing Harlequin romances, pop ballads, and screenplays for various Meg Ryan films. Finally liberated by a nation addicted to Oprah's brand of feel-goodism, Kyron is now revealing such groundbreaking messages as "love is the universe's most powerful force" at an unrivaled pace.

"You're not going to believe this," I told Meredith over the telephone, trying to figure out a delicate way to phrase my findings. "But I think that indigo stuff is . . . not true."

"Let me guess. Jesus told you that?"

I'd already ruined more than one gathering when Meredith was present—like the time I couldn't hide my astonishment at the details of a lesbian sleepover or when marijuana paraphernalia was pulled out of mothers' purses at playgroup. I could tell by Meredith's voice that the novelty of my Christianity was beginning to wear thin. It struck me as odd, though, that Meredith assumed I was rejecting the indigo children idea—out of all the possible reasons—because Christians like me don't accept "science." By this time, we'd hung out quite a bit, discussing politics, fashion, and the dietary benefit of cow colostrum. I had frequently run up against her presuppositions about conservatives, which led to many conversations about gay rights, race issues, and exactly why "Peter, Paul, and Mary" were in the Bible. We'd laughed, eaten freshly baked challah, and even had Yiddish lessons. But I was beginning to realize the chasm between us was too great even for Kyron to bridge.

I told Meredith the origins of the indigo nonsense, and I even made the (I thought) sensible point that alien abductions, pagan god channeling, and psychic connections did not exactly fit within MIT's definition of science. She was unmoved. I suppose the indigo child explanation was one she liked—one that made her feel her child was special, and so that was that. There was nothing more to say. To Meredith, my Christianity rendered me a hopeless fanatic and enemy of scientific progress, while her paganism made her, well, open-minded.

Our previous conversations used to be exciting, full of hope that perhaps we could understand and bridge these huge cultural gaps. But after this one, I suddenly realized why Meredith had previously enjoyed talking to me: she thought I might be changing, that she was opening my eyes to new truths. When she realized that in fact I was just being both shocked and curious—that I wasn't dropping Jesus for Kyron—everything changed. Her voice grew cold and bleak, and I knew our budding friendship had suffered a grievous blow.

As I hung up the phone, I heard Zoe screaming in the background.

Politics

An election!? That's one of those deals where they close the bars, isn't it?

—*Barney Gumbel, from* The Simpsons

M.O.B. Mentality

"WANT TO KICK Bush out of office?"

I heard this as I walked around Philadelphia during the 2004 election season almost as frequently as I heard my kids wail the plaintive "Mommmy!" when they were upset, happy, hurt, tired, or just plain bored. Once, on a late-September trek from our apartment to church (a distance of twelve city blocks), we counted eleven requests to either vote for Kerry, volunteer for Kerry, or name our next child Kerry. While I was amazed at their efforts, David was encouraged, believing Kerry's efforts must be faltering if the Democrats couldn't actually get activists working *all twelve* blocks.

At first I smiled and simply responded, "No thank you," but my politeness wasn't reciprocated by the young Democratic activists. So, by August, my responses turned into the more specific and intentionally annoying, "We support President Bush"—which was met with boos, hisses, and occasional weeping and gnashing of teeth. My benevolence toward the canvassers that day decreased with every step, so that by the time we made it to church, my responses had degenerated from the cold but polite to the downright belligerent. Only a good sermon on grace and forgiveness could enable me to make it home without engaging in a fistfight.

At one particular intersection, a man held up a homemade sign that proclaimed "33 days till we CHANGE THE WORLD!" A "36" had been crossed out with a marker, as had "35," "34," and so forth. And so my autumn ticked away day by day on a giant piece of cardboard over the head of a guy who apparently had nothing better to do than receive car-honking approbation from Subarus with bumpers proclaiming "Hate Is NOT a Family Value."

Knowing my own limitations, I tried my best not to engage the voter registration people without David around. He was a calming force, his very presence allowing me to feel less isolated in the blue world . . . less like a cornered animal.

Once, after the young men wearing matching T-shirts heard my drawl (or my politeness and deduced I wasn't local), they looked at each other knowingly, as if the crime lab had come back with a fingerprint match. They knew, or thought they knew, a great deal more about me.

"You're from a red state, aren't you?"

Now, I'd like to report I stopped the stroller and explained how my conservatism is not the product of my Southern culture, how my political views have been shaped by observation and scrutiny. "I could be liberal—I'm from Al Gore's home state," I could've said. Instead, not wanting to subject the kids to yet another political discussion and not trusting my ability to sustain a casual conversation, I smiled and said, "Yep."

And that was enough explanation until I turned the corner

and faced another gaggle of people armed with the artillery of clipboards and smug, condescending faces.

"Help get rid of Bush?"

Amid the onslaught, I decided to get a conservative T-shirt, a sort of cotton kryptonite that might ward off these pearly smiles and pleading inquiries. Since moving to Philadelphia, I'd seen numerous liberal shirts, including one with a picture of Reagan that read "Vote Republican, Where Senility Is a Virtue." Another said succinctly "Evil GOP Bastards." And then there was the ever-popular "Buck Fush." I could exercise my free speech as well, I thought—I had an upper torso and a Visa card.

"You can't order that," my husband said when he saw me browsing the Internet late one night. The shirt in question read "Keep America Safe for Terrorists: Vote Kerry."

"It's too inflammatory," he said. "And not that one either," as he pointed to my other favorite: "Moore Is a Big, Fat Liar." I explained how I wanted to repel the persistent voter registration activists, and I threw in some philosophical stuff about Philadelphia being the birthplace of freedom and how we had an obligation to exercise our First Amendment rights.

"You wear those shirts and it'll be like wearing a bull's-eye on your chest. Conservative T-shirts have to be self-deprecating and funny. Otherwise, people think you're mean."

He was right. If I seemed too religious or conservative, I'd be pushed to the fringes of society as a presumed knuckle-dragging, gap-toothed redneck. Since I still wanted to be invited to parties and shop with friends, I camouflaged myself as a liberal—Birkenstocks, peasant skirts, unwashed hair, and unshaven legs (though, admittedly, those last two were due to occasional bouts of laziness). Most of all, I avoided appearing "judgmental." My main tool for survival was the ambiguous facial expression, which enabled me to avoid agreeing or disagreeing in any way. For example, when I complained that a cashier didn't give me correct change, my friend said, "Well, my astrologist said the planets are not aligned this week, so it's not surprising." I quickly learned the best way to deal with statements like this was a look of utter ambiguity, so they couldn't tell if I was agreeing with them, judging them, or just plain constipated. I perfected it with many hours of practice in the mirror, like I used to practice kissing. My eyebrows shot up (as if interested), I smiled (as if amused), then looked away (as if bored), all in a fraction of a second. I used it at the park, when a mom chastised her daughter for taking another girl's doll: "Emma, is that the best way to avoid bad karma?"

A blue city is a social minefield for the conservative who reveals the first signs of political incorrectness. So for weeks on end I rolled my stroller around town, carefully hiding my true beliefs lest someone incorrectly conclude I was a homophobe, warmonger, or racist. I got my hair cut at a salon under a gigantic sign maligning President Bush. At playgroup, I kept my mouth closed as the parents at the park talked about the "war for oil." When I dropped my daughter off at kindergarten, I deftly navigated between the mothers who wore buttons proclaiming "I'm a member of the M.O.B.—Mothers Opposing Bush." When I walked around town, I passed stacks of alternative papers that read "Vote for Kerry or Burn in Hell."

The rhetoric was inescapable. On a tour of a public elementary school I was considering for Camille, I noticed an entire wall of unflattering drawings of President Bush, with captions like "People hate George Bush because he lies" and "John Kerry is an honest man, but George Bush is a coward" written in large, childish handwriting.

Even grocery shopping during the election was laced with political overtones. In Whole Foods, nine out of ten shoppers had Kerry stickers on their Birkenstocks or Nader tattoos on the smalls of their backs. When I brought home some freshly ground organic peanut butter, my husband noticed the Whole Foods logo and said, "You're half the way to voting Democrat."

"Well, where do Republicans shop?" I asked.

He looked at me as if I had lost my mind. "Super Wal-Mart, of course."

It was just my luck that when Election Day finally came, my apartment building happened to be a polling station. Hundreds of voters lined up, blocking my exit from the building and making it impossible to push my double stroller through the doors. "Excuse me, do you mind letting me through?" I asked politely. From the middle of the crowd a man's voice shouted above the others, "Why don't you go back to the red state you left? Your vote won't count here."

I'd been pushed around enough. So I went back up to my apartment, got a "W" sticker intended for a vehicle's bumper, and stuck it on my shoulder before running my errands. By the end of the day, I'd verbally sparred with a lesbian group campaigning on the streets, called the Election Commission on MoveOn.org for illegally asking me questions as I voted, and retaliated to dozens of sidewalk insults. Three pedestrians made eye contact with me and smiled, which I took to mean they were either secretly Republican or amused at my futile attempt at free speech.

By that afternoon, misleading exit polls were flying all over the news, and giddy people stood on the corners of the downtown streets with professionally made signs proclaiming "VICTORY!" Philadelphia ended up voting 82 percent for Kerry, narrowly putting Pennsylvania into the Democrats' blue territory. Slowly, however, the cold hard truth of the national election results began to sink in for the Philadelphians, and a sense of utter shock settled over the city.

I didn't gloat. In fact, I never mentioned a word. Conservatives living in blue cities have to blend in, be extremely kind, and have the wisdom to know when to keep their mouths shut. I did finally pick a T-shirt—it said "Even on Drugs—Rush Is Right," but I never worked up enough righteous anger to wear it. Now it sits in my drawer wondering what it did to deserve the same fate as my pleather skirt, leg warmers, and shirts with shoulder pads that make me look like Dick Butkus.

But You Seem So Reasonable

WHILE I WOULD argue with random liberals on the street, I always kept my conservatism close to my chest when it came to relationships. Being a Republican was a deal breaker; we all knew that—kind of like picking your nose at red lights or stealing tips off restaurant tables. Only Rene and Meredith knew the truth, and, quite frankly, justifying myself to them had become a full-time job. I liked to think of my GOP bent as my alter ego, the smart, conservative superhero itching to burst forth any second to dispel the convoluted beliefs of my new blue state acquaintances. I was waiting for just the right moment to dazzle the ladies at the park or the mothers at Camille's school with my logic or impress them with my homespun moral values.

But my coming out didn't happen exactly as I'd scripted. I sat one day with some mothers on the benches that face each other in the middle of Three Bears Park—coveted see-and-be-seen seats—where fashionable mothers gab while their kids play nonviolent, character-affirming games in one of Philly's best neighborhoods.

Suddenly one of the ladies mentioned she'd heard I was writing a column for the Philadelphia *City Paper*, and all ears perked. "What do you write about?"

"Oh, I write from a red state point of view, to show readers there's life outside the big city." I used a folksy voice to come off as charming instead of conservative.

But they were no fools. Claudia Shipman, who was still proudly wearing her Mothers Opposing Bush button weeks after Kerry's defeat, spoke first. "Are you saying, you're a—" not even wanting to say the word "Republican" aloud. She said it in a hushed tone like some people say the F word.

This was my big moment. As casually as possible, I told her I voted for Bush *and* supported the war on terror. I braced myself for a heated debate on Saddam and for barbed comments including the word "strategery." I mentally ran through a few speaking points I'd gotten off National Review Online and dug in my heels in anticipation.

Claudia's only response was a rather dejected "But you seem so *reasonable*."

The other mothers exchanged worried glances before averting their eyes. I had hoped to trigger an exciting give-and-take, but instead it felt like I had popped a balloon—things just deflated. I think they would have been happier had I proclaimed I was a pedophile on the prowl. Instead, I felt like I'd tricked them into liking one of the prickliest, most off-putting creatures on the planet—a conservative.

To their credit, they handled it with as much grace as they could muster. "You have to meet *Louise*," they all said in unison. Evidently there was one other lady in the entire city of Philadelphia who was Republican. "She's not mean, though," they clarified.

Several weeks later, I was sitting in Louise's Delancey Street home, drinking coffee at one of her weekly get-togethers with local women. She introduced herself with a flourish, and I could instantly see how Democrats would overlook her archaic beliefs. She was bright and cheery—a former Philadelphia 76ers cheer-leader—confidently offering coffee in mismatched mugs while women casually passed in and out of her kitchen.

"Look what someone gave me! Isn't this a riot?" she said upon meeting me. She plopped down a book, *Dumb Things That Democrats Have Said,* right on the place mat in front of me. "I thought you'd get a kick out of it."

As she flittered around, greeting people who'd dropped in late, I was thrilled to be there—an urban setting where smart women of diverse opinions meet to talk. City life couldn't get any better than this. I was prepared to meet all my new friends, people who would embrace me and spend hours discussing issues of the day. Months from now we'd be shopping at Tiffany's, and one of them would turn to me and say, "I knew from the first time I saw you at Louise's you were the kind of person I wanted to know."

I snapped out of my reverie when I realized, with horror, that my new friends were entering the room, taking one glance at the book before me, and hurrying to the farthest corner of the room. Louise had left it right in front of me, the social equivalent of having gloppy Kleenexes on your lap. If the book had been titled *The Sadomasochist Handbook* I'd have gotten a warmer reception. I flipped through it nonchalantly and smiled a disapproving smile. That gosh-darn Louise, I tried to convey. Always joking. But my friendship prospects were disappearing every second the book was visible. I considered slipping it into my purse, but I thought theft might be considered gauche.

Finally Claudia walked through the door, greeted me, and noticed the book. "'Dumb Things Democrats Have Said,'" she read in a stage whisper, before smiling condescendingly.

"Bringing books like that here will not win you any friends. If you want to be invited back, I'd suggest leaving the propaganda at home."

I smiled, choosing to act like it was a joke; I didn't want to incriminate the kind hostess who was obliviously adding cream to people's coffee.

Another lady chimed in, "You're smiling because you think we're kidding. Trust me"—she narrowed her eyes and lowered her voice—"we're not."

"I'm not smiling because I think you're kidding," I said, hoping to lighten the mood. "I'm just surprised this book isn't longer." It went over like a Chappaquiddick joke at a Kennedy house.

Louise, realizing what was going on, grabbed the book and moved the talk away from politics. But no matter how friendly the conversation seemed after that, everyone knew. I'd been warned.

Tension escalated among my friends when I began writing more articles for the *City Paper*, a free alternative weekly distributed in orange boxes across the city, funded by large pictures of hot Latina lovers or young black stallions in the back pages. Nearly half a million people read it each week, thumbing through the F-word-sprinkled pages to find an apartment, a gay massage parlor, or new reasons to hate President Bush—all in one convenient tabloid.

Miraculously, the editor had commissioned me to write short opinion pieces from my "red state" point of view, which ensured the Letters to the Editor section was always full of angry missives from liberals who liked their news without the bothersome inconvenience of disagreement.

One column drew more hate mail than the others, because I'd done the unpardonable—suggested materials that promote what I perceived to be the "gay agenda" shouldn't be taught in a public school kindergarten class.

The letters started rolling in. For weeks, the Letters to the Editor section was stuffed with notes suggesting I go back to the South, that I was a "Holy Roller who does not have a direct line to heaven," that I was using the *City Paper* as a "tool of my bigotry," and that I was, ahem, a neo-Nazi b——. One advertiser even pulled his ads from the paper, and I was nicknamed "Our Lady of Constant Moral Logorrhea."

The insults honestly started to get to me. At first I was eager to see if an article had touched a nerve, but eventually I had to stop reading the paper altogether. The sting of the barbs had grown stronger than the pleasure of being published. So I avoided the orange boxes on every street corner and even averted my eyes when I saw people reading it on the bus or at a diner. One day, after I had successfully dodged the paper for an entire week, my husband walked into the apartment holding the latest edition, opened to the Letters to the Editor page. I sensed compassion in his eyes as he leaned in and kissed me on the cheek. I was so fortunate to have David, my one ally in this liberal city. "Do you know what you are?" he whispered in my ear, his breath warming me to my toes. A courageous soul unafraid to stand up against political correctness? I wondered. A brave mom capable of causing an uproar? I postulated.

"'A s——t-head warmonger,'" he quoted from the Letters section before bursting into hysterical laughter. "It says so right here." He thumped the page.

Criticism from strangers was bad enough, and I quickly tired of the barbed comments from acquaintances in the park as well. Thankfully, my closest friends were Rene and Meredith, who seemed to accept me in spite of my absolute refusal to recycle. In return for their overlooking my character flaws, I never brought up the phrase "indigo children" again. We'd entered into a peaceful, although seemingly mismatched relationship. On Mother's Day, I ran a 5K for a breast cancer foundation in honor of my mother and was exhausted by the time I made it to Meredith's house for brunch. We'd begun a Sunday tradition involving free-trade coffee, homemade muffins, and the best organic cantaloupes money can buy. David and I especially looked forward to spending time on a pleasant weekly basis with what had become our core group of friends.

However, as soon as we set foot in Meredith's five-thousand-square-foot home, I immediately realized something was wrong.

"I heard about your article," Meredith said instead of giving me the usual kiss on the cheek. "Why are you so prejudiced against gays anyway?" I paused, taking a hot cup of coffee from Rene, and tried to figure out what I'd missed. We'd talked about gay rights many times before but the gleam of contempt in her eye was new.

Meredith's husband, Seth, and Rene's husband, Adam, are good-natured and enjoyable guys, educated and funny. That day, however, I couldn't shake the feeling we'd been ambushed—it seemed like we'd walked into a roomful of people who'd been discussing us seconds before but who lacked the good Southern manners to change the subject and feign affection anyway.

Normally an instigator, Adam acted as an ambassador for peace, rephrasing our arguments with slightly altered meanings to see if either of us found them more palatable. But the more we talked, the worse it got. For hours, the heated and sometimes vitriolic comments weren't being deflected with my usual charm and good nature. It was like I'd lost my superpowers. We analyzed the situation from every possible angle, but nothing ever seemed to help.

"I don't know why we can't discuss this rationally without you losing your temper," Meredith said, after the conversation had thankfully drifted off topic.

"I'm not angry."

"Look at the way you're sitting—your arms crossed and back to me. Everyone knows those are unspoken signals of rejection."

Truthfully, I was trying not to cry. I'm not sure if it was my long morning run or the weeks of constant criticism, but I was officially weary and dangerously close to losing it.

I uncrossed my arms in a dramatic gesture, turned my chair to Meredith, and threw my head in her lap, hoping the absurdity of the situation would dawn on us and we'd share a laugh about it at next week's brunch. Meredith smoothed my hair with her hands and smiled.

The effect was short-lived. Soon I was accusing her of stereotyping me, and she was questioning me about my sexual past, whether I'd had women lovers, and suggesting I send my kids to Christian schools if I wanted to shelter them so much.

When the table was cleared and the coffee was cold, it eventually came down to this. Meredith looked at me and said, "Your beliefs are so dangerously obsolete, they should be silenced."

"You're forgetting the small detail that conservatives have constitutional rights."

"The Constitution should be amended."

And so I sat there, exhausted from my run, hoping against hope the tears forming in my eyes didn't spill out onto the table linens. She ended the conversation and our friendship by saying she didn't want to discuss this further because my status as a Christian meant I lacked the mental skills to have an intelligent debate. Her last words spoken to me were "You only believe in faith," she said, "not logic." At that moment, the child who may or may not be an alien ambled through the room, exuding her indigo aura, and dropped crumbs on the floor.

The Blind Date

WHEN I LIVED in Kentucky, I was invited to join a book club that met every month at a local restaurant famous for brunch. I took notes in the margins of my book and prepared discussion questions for our first gathering, but it turned out my friends were more impressed by the croissants than the recollections of an aged geisha.

In an effort to find people interested in books and the writing life, I joined an online writers group. Initially, I was apprehensive about the whole thing—any of the several hundred members could send e-mails to my account about various topics only writers cared about: query letters, correct spacing, agents, and double-coupon days at Save-A-Lot. Over time, I developed friendships with the other writers (whom I knew mostly by screen names) and looked forward to e-mails from "Spyder," "Stephie143," and "RomanceChick" even if I wouldn't recognize them seated next to me on an airplane.

Eventually the group swelled to over a thousand members and included best-selling novelists, newspaper columnists, and erotica writers. The group got so large that members in the same cities began meeting at restaurants for dinner and discussion of the craft, which sounded very appealing to me. I imagined smoky dives, invigorating book discussions, and advice on opening paragraphs exchanged artfully over hot food and cold drinks. But since no one in the group was from central Kentucky, I contented myself with what I read about the events and continued working in isolation.

When David got a job in Philadelphia, however, I sent out an invitation immediately to everyone in the area. Within the week, I had a response from three people who were interested. I envisioned CoolCopyChick as a secretary with a short skirt, a gaping camisole, and a pencil sticking out of her messily gathered hair, who turned the Xerox aspect of her job into an ironic statement about the corporate culture. Judging by their screen names, I figured writing partners BFlyHugs and BFlySmiles shared their Care Bears in elementary school, and bet they dotted their *i*'s with hearts and smiley faces.

We decided to meet at seven o'clock at Jones Restaurant, a block from my apartment. To be honest, I was a little nervous. How would I recognize them?

I composed an e-mail to my three Philadelphia counterparts, suggesting we describe ourselves in advance. "I'll be wearing a red rose in my lapel," I typed, inspired by a story I'd heard about a soldier who'd fallen in love with a pen pal during World War II. When he finally returned from Europe, she asked him to meet her. "You'll recognize me," she wrote, "by the red rose I'll be wearing on my lapel." When the soldier arrived at their meeting place, a svelte young woman in a green suit walked by him . . . but no rose. Behind her was an elderly lady with a rose on her crumpled lapel. He approached the older lady, disappointed but thankful for her encouraging letters, and asked, "May I take you to dinner?" As the story goes, the old woman smiled. "I don't know what this is about, son," she answered, "but the lady in the green suit begged me to wear this rose on my lapel, and said if you asked me to dinner, I should tell you she's waiting for you at the diner across the street."

Likewise, I was hoping my urban writer friends would befriend me in spite of my unpopular political beliefs, delving beneath the harsh Republican exterior to find a heart of gold—doing for conservatives what Julia Roberts had done for prostitutes. I paused before sending the e-mail, however, when I realized I didn't actually own a garment with lapels. Conjuring the perfect symbol for our blossoming friendship, I composed another e-mail: "You'll recognize me by the carefully chosen book I'll be holding."

I tried to think of what book would make the perfect statement about who I was. The Bible? Jennifer Weiner's *Good in Bed*? But before I worked myself into a tizzy, I received a short message from BFlyHugs: "Let's just meet by the hostess stand."

I could already tell that, although they obviously lacked a flair for the dramatic, we'd be instant friends.

Wednesday, November 3, turned out to be a historic day, and not just because I finally was able to hang out with other writers. It just so happened that on that particular morning—after one of the most contentious presidential elections in memory—John Kerry conceded the election to George W. Bush. Emotions were raw, and Philadelphians were walking around the city looking like their dogs had been shot. The day before, misleading exit polls had caused jubilant Philadelphians to cele-brate prematurely. But after the concession, the atmosphere was less festive than at a funeral.

I hadn't said a word about it. All of the trash talking and pre-election bickering came to an abrupt halt, and an eerie quiet set-tled over pedestrians still wearing Kerry campaign buttons as they walked to work. I, of course, was thrilled that the election was finally over. I'd already lost one friend over political and philosophical differences, and the conversations in the park were getting so impassioned I feared the children might pick up the adults' profanity. That day, the spirit of disappointment hung heavily over the city, but it was not going to ruin my first night out with my new friends.

When we all got there, there were no crumpled lapels, roses, or green suits, but I detected telltale signs of liberalism—BFly-Smiles wore Euroglasses, the thickly framed Steven Soderbergh types that just scream "keep your rosaries off my ovaries," and BFlyHugs drove a Volkswagen. As we talked, they mentioned that they had met in college and had roomed together for ten years. I hadn't realized that they shared the "BFly" portion of their screen names in much the same way married people con-solidate last names.

I didn't pry.

CoolCopyChick wasn't how I envisioned her, either. A pas-tor's wife from the suburbs, she had red permed hair and wore a green V-necked sweater and khaki pants. Her screen name was a play off her last name, which, it turns out, was Cool.

As the BFlies settled on one side of the table and we sat down on the other, it felt like we were being punk'd. When our secret identities were revealed (they were—surprise!—leftist liberal feminists, and we were both—surprise!—Republican Christians), I figured this would be a long night. Perhaps everyone sensed the potential for disaster, because we immediately agreed not to talk about politics.

"So what do you write?" BFlyHugs asked the pastor's wife.

"Articles about Christian social activism." Had I not been next to the window I would've sprinted toward the door. The perpetual political tension of the election had worn me down to the point of near exhaustion; I didn't know if I could take one more night.

However, it soon became apparent that not talking about the election on that day was like playing the don't-step-on-a-crack game as a child—you could pull it off, but not gracefully. It's almost like we've forgotten how to disagree amicably. Sociologists have discovered that even though racial segregation has been declining over the past couple of decades, self-imposed political segregation by party affiliation has increased by 47 percent. Increased mobility means you're less likely to fight with your neighbor about politics, because it's less likely that you'll ever disagree.[1] We bucked the trend that night, as CoolCopy-Chick talked about her Christian writing and the election loomed larger and larger in the background. Eventually, sensing we could no longer avoid it, we delved right into the heart of politics.

We discussed the offensive behavior of the religious activists at a recent gay pride parade—a group of Christians were holding signs with Scripture, shouting at an obviously flustered transvestite speaker . . . presumably under the spiritual obligation to

annoy people into the kingdom of heaven. And then we talked
about my experience voting when a Democrat had chased me
across the lobby of the voting area, loudly wondering if my politics were due to a troubled childhood.

They apologized to us, and we apologized to them—which
oddly was very meaningful, even though it was apology by proxy.
Then we talked about our pasts. I told them my first job was
waiting tables at a Huddle House (similar to a Waffle House but
not as classy) and that my husband's was selling guns at Wal-
Mart. They told us about venturing into the South one weekend
and how they were identified as Northeasterners without even
opening their mouths. It was fascinating to explore how our respective cultural experiences had molded our political perspectives.

No voices were raised, no arguments made. The main ingredient of the evening, in fact, was laughter, as the tension dissipated like celebrities after a Republican win.

"In normal circumstances, I doubt we'd all be having dinner," I commented as dessert and coffee were being served. The
BFlies laughed and admitted they'd never had a conversation
with two evangelical Christians before. In fact, they didn't even
know any.

Which gets to the heart of the matter. The image most
urban liberals have of red state America is far from accurate—
usually more of a caricature pieced together from countless
clichés than based on any real relationships. It's shocking that
there's more philosophical diversity in Grundy County, Tennessee, than in our nation's capital. My parents' hometown in
the foothills of the Appalachians voted solidly for . . . John

Kerry, 57 percent compared to 43 percent for Bush. There were even nineteen lonely voters who defiantly cast hopeless votes for Nader, which didn't even add up to one percentage point. However, in Washington, D.C., Manhattan, and Philadelphia, 80 to 90 percent of voters pulled the lever for Kerry,[2] which made me feel like the subject of a *National Geographic* special ("The conservative is a breed rarely seen in this part of the country—some hope this species will become extinct by 2008. If I hide behind the soda display, I might be able to get some footage of this conservative shopping. Yes, see her pick up the Wonder bread? It's not organic, it's not whole grain, and it's not . . . even . . . on . . . sale").

This amazing political segregation reminded me of the stories of racial segregation where my parents grew up. When she was a girl, my mom went to the country store to pick up a five-gallon tub of ice cream packed in dry ice and brought in on a truck. It was the Fourth of July, they'd ordered chocolate, and she'd been looking forward to that day for months. But she forgot about the ice cream when she saw the man who was unloading the truck. She stood there and gawked at him, the first black person she'd ever seen.

That evening at Jones, the ice in our glasses of tea melted and left watery rings on the table. I think the BFlies were feeling a little like my mother did back then, shocked at seeing the hearts and thoughts of people so different from them for the first time. And we were having fun as well. It turns out, they aren't gay—just "dangerously codependent"—and CoolCopyChick ended up confessing she'd voted for Al Gore in 2000. We lingered around the credit card receipts for quite some time and drained our glasses to the lemon wedges. I wondered if Jones Restaurant used some sort of magical ingredient in the food that erased partisan pettiness. I left my new friends reluctantly, afraid the spell would be broken, and hesitant to return to the aftermath of Kerry's concession. On the way out the door, BFlyHugs commented that dinner with us after the decisive Bush victory was just what she needed—a window into the red state world that wasn't as frightening as they previously believed—and we made it a point to get together every few months for dinner. Living in Philly was a constant test of wills and politics. Sometimes the mixture was an explosive disaster and sometimes it was an interesting pleasure. The total unpredictability of it all is what made it a fun and sometimes prickly adventure.

Suffice it to say, however, that after I had dreamed of having the kind of night I never had in Kentucky, the evening with CoolCopyChick and the BFlies certainly didn't disappoint.

Life

Cloquet hated reality but realized it was still the only place to get a good steak.

—*Woody Allen*

Uncivil Disobedience

FOR THE FIRST seven years of marriage, David and I didn't keep track of our checks or ATM withdrawals. Whatever financial penalty we incurred from unnoticed bank errors, we just counted as the cost of freedom. After one too many bounced checks, however, David bought a computer checkbook program to bring some organization to our lives. But when the technological novelty wore off, he turned over the sole responsibility to me, which was like giving a toddler a chessboard and being surprised when he eats it. My jaunt as financial planner lasted until the phones were disconnected, and David's next turn ended when he realized he couldn't mail the bills due to a lack of stamps. The pendulum of financial responsibility has swung back and forth so many times, it's hard to know who's more inept. (Although David is certain the distinction belongs to me after I bounced our *tithe check* at church.)

Our laziness extends to other areas of life as well. When a lightbulb goes out, we'll sit in the dark for months, wearing mismatched socks and putting Preparation H on our toothbrushes until one of us caves in. Additionally, David has been known to pass by Blockbuster with a video sitting on the passenger seat, just to avoid making a left turn. He thinks, Would I pay three dollars to not have to return this video right at this moment? Of course, it never was *just* three dollars. In fact, we're the reason the company got rid of late fees. They got so rich off David, they decided to let the rest of America slide. Once David sold his Honda Accord only to have the new owner call us a week later saying she'd found a *Reversal of Fortune* tape in the trunk.

But our laziness took a turn for the illegal when we moved to Ithaca. After the movers unloaded our last box, we found a Welcome to Ithaca packet sitting on the kitchen counter featuring historical sketches of interesting locales, colorful guides to area gorges, and a segment on recycling laws that made *Anna Karenina* look comparatively succinct. Apparently, the political leaders of Ithaca had decided in 1992 that residents of Tompkins County should not only be required to recycle newspaper, cans, glass bottles, jars, and corrugated cardboard but also "strongly encouraged" to recycle mixed paper, boxboard, plastic bottles and jugs, and used toilet paper. This suggestion didn't take the form of a nice note in the mailbox or a pleasant public service announcement on the radio. It was "encouraged" in the same way that Al Gore could be described as charismatic or water as dry. In reality, they *taxed* every bag of garbage thrown away.

The way it worked was simple. Every bag of garbage had to be tagged with little fluorescent green stickers that were sold at grocery stores for about as much as a semester of Ivy League education. Recycling, however, was free. And the encouragement worked. I met one woman who composted and recycled so much she threw away only one bag of trash per year.

I tried valiantly to figure out the recycling codes and bought all the containers required to properly sort all the waste materials. In the process, the kids had to live in the garage to make room for all the bins.

But when my parents came to visit from Tennessee, I realized my whole system was going down in a ball of flames. They had only a few days to visit, and I wasn't going to spend half of them lecturing them on washing SpaghettiO remnants out of tin cans. While I never really thought about it before, my mother has always been a natural recycler . . . at least of some items. Thanks to her, not a single cardboard box will ever find its way back into society—she guards them like a junkie protects a cocaine stash. This meant at Christmas, we'd rip the bow off a big box reading CD Player only to find a lint brush or a value pack of toothbrushes. She saves boxes of various sizes that can accommodate anything from fine china to a dead body, and she'd take just as much joy at providing either. Box hoarding, for me, defines motherhood just as much as does the art of creating one long snake of an apple peel.

But by the end of their visit, my Jeep was packed with garbage bags containing diapers, glass bottles, and Tide containers—all mixed decadently together. My garbage bags were in the back of the Jeep because, well, I was out of garbage tags. No garbage tags, no garbage pickup. So I had to load a week's worth of garbage into the back of an SUV and drive ten miles to the dump. Actually, it wasn't a dump at all. Dumps are those glorious places located outside Southern towns, managed by a guy named Ag with flies buzzing around his head. He scratches himself while you cleanse yourself of the trash in your life and perhaps find some cool old furniture. Ithaca, however, had a "waste management center," which took itself way too seriously. It had loftier goals than being a mere dump, such as saving the planet. There were no Ags there. Just "peace officers" (guards who didn't carry weapons) maintaining the delicate balance of the universe by not throwing away garbage that could be recycled into inferior, more expensive products.

The smell was so bad I almost vomited twice before making it there. I was pregnant with Austin at the time, and almost everything nauseated me—including the aroma of my daughter's week-old diapers and half-eaten chicken legs.

In the towns I've lived in in the South, recycling was simplified to a spray-painted green pickup truck that stopped by the house once a month to pick up old newspapers. But Ithaca's waste management center was a brand-new, gleaming structure off Commercial Avenue, sitting proudly on the earth it was saving.

I was a little nervous. I knew it was against the law to throw away milk jugs, but I figured I could appeal to the compassion of the guards. But when I got to the gate, my head sticking out the window to breathe in the crisp December air, I realized the plant closed at four o'clock. Not five. Apparently, environmentally aware city workers don't need to work a full day. I was fifteen minutes late.

I had no idea what to do. Fighting off the nausea, I saw my only chance—an unlocked gate in the chain-link fence. I got out of the Jeep, calmly unhitched the gate, and drove right into the waste plant like it was noon. Being pregnant was definitely uncomfortable, but at least you got some sympathy and respect. When the guards saw my huge belly, I figured, they'd cut me some slack.

Immediately, in my rearview mirror, I saw men in orange vests running after my Jeep, arms flailing like they were trying to get the attention of a lifeguard.

Through my open window, I heard, "Stop! You're trespassing on government property!"

I made it to the section of the center where unsorted garbage was dumped. While the bottle-recycling section was marked by a green sign reading "Glass," and the can section with a green sign reading "Metal," this section sported a skull and crossbones superimposed over an image of a desolate planet. I'd found my mark. The guards were gaining on me, so I defied the heft of my pregnant body, jumping out of the Jeep and tossing the bags into the dump. I got one in. Two. Then . . .

"Do *not* drop the bag!"

I froze.

"You are trespassing and illegally disposing of waste material." They looked closely at my bags, and I wished I'd splurged on the expensive, opaque kind. "Is that a soda bottle I see in there?" He looked at me like he'd just discovered heroin.

"I'm going to have to ask you to back away from the refuse site."

I stood there holding the bag over the dump like a loan shark dangling a guy off a balcony by his ankles. While it hovered in the air, I stuck out my pregnant belly and explained that my parents didn't understand the recycling laws; I even almost cried. But the men did not relent.

"If you drop that bag, we'll have to call the police."

As I stood there, all the absurdities and indignities caused by my sheer laziness flashed through my mind—the phone service being cut off, not taking the kids to the library because of accumulated late fines, and realizing I hadn't paid the credit card bill by the look of embarrassment on a cashier's face. But my shame was overpowered by something else—brave defiance in the face of environmental totalitarianism. My bag of garbage would not cause one single glacier to shrink, nor would a single hurricane form because a milk jug wrongfully wound up in a landfill. The stink of the garbage was overcome by the stink of political correctness. I wasn't dropping garbage. I was liberating America.

"Then do it," I said.

And with that word, I dropped the last bag into the great abyss. I was surprised they didn't call the cops and even more surprised they didn't dive in after it. So I waddled off, secure in the knowledge that I was joining Jefferson, Franklin, Adams, and Washington in the pantheon of the heroes of liberty.

These Y'all's?

DAVID AND I uprooted our family and moved to an apartment that we'd never actually seen nine hundred miles away. Since we were both inundated with work, making a trip to Tennessee just to see an apartment (which, after all, looked perfectly fine over the Internet) seemed superfluous. Plus, we planned on living there for only as long as it took to build a home on a farm south of town. We signed a one-year lease the apartment manager kindly faxed us and forgot about it until moving day.

I think it was somewhere in West Virginia that I began to worry. The movers had taken our belongings, the kids were sleeping in their car seats, and suddenly the possibility of absolute disaster loomed ominously in my mind. You'd think that after all our relocations, we'd have the process down to a science, but our aversion to planning trumped our hard-won moving experience. I have to admit it felt pretty foolish to have to MapQuest our own address.

To make matters worse, David had just discovered that he had to be in Phoenix for business on the day the furniture was expected to arrive. Although we were driving to Tennessee together, the logistics of moving in fell squarely on my shoulders. I closed my eyes to catch some sleep while we sped down the interstate, images of rats and leaky faucets dancing in my mind.

The next morning when we drove into the complex, we sighed in relief. The neighborhood was nice enough, the buildings were new, and the apartment manager graciously offered to tell us about all the nice churches nearby. The apartment smelled of new carpet and fresh paint, more pleasant to me than Chanel No. 5. I'd been living in a musty hundred-year-old building for so long that our new home's economy GE appliances, neutral paint color, and nondescript white cabinets elated me. Okay, so maybe it was a tad smaller than our previous place. As I tried to mentally arrange our furniture in the room, it slowly dawned on me that we had a space problem.

Make that, *I* had a problem—while we slept on the floor that night, David was ordering room service in Arizona. So the next morning I rented a nearby storage unit, but the man at the front desk warned me, "Unit 27 isn't close to the road, so you better be sure your movers will carry your stuff that far from the gate." He had a point. My movers weren't obligated to do any of this. After making a mental note to get lots of cash from the ATM for bribes, I thanked him and began to back out the door.

"Don't you want to see the unit?" he asked. This man obviously didn't know who he was dealing with. If I hadn't investigated living quarters for my own children, I certainly wouldn't scope out a storage space.

"Suit yourself," he said. "But be outta here by closing time. That electronic gate turns off every night at seven o'clock. That code on your receipt will open it up, but if you're in there after hours you might as well get comfortable," he said, "'cause you ain't gettin' out till the mornin'."

I hadn't heard anyone say "ain't" in a long time. I remembered my fourth grade teacher in Kentucky writing it in bold capital letters on the chalkboard. She said, with a wink, "Y'all know this ain't a word, right?" There, she used "ain't" instead of the proper "is not," but it's versatile enough to also substitute for "am" and "not." For example, you'd say, "He is renting a storage unit, isn't he?" but never "I am renting the unit, amn't I?" To avoid the ungainly contraction for "am not," we are taught from an early age to say the wildly illogical "aren't I?" but never its grammatical equivalent, "I are not." Hearing the cashier say "ain't" seemed a testimony to the practicality of Southern expressions, and it made me happy in spite of its inelegance.

By the time I arrived back home, a man named Sarge and his crew were already unloading furniture. The boxes stacked high and deep within the eighteen-wheeler made me wonder if they'd accidentally mixed our shipment up with Paris Hilton's shoes.

I sat on top of the kitchen counter with a checklist to make sure all the 160 boxes arrived and to tell the movers where to place each box—but even from that vantage point I could tell there was a civil war brewing among the workers. The moving company was from Brooklyn, and they had hired Tennessee guys to help unload locally. As the New Yorkers barked orders at the slower-paced Southerners, resentment was obviously brewing underneath the surface.

"If all Northerners are like them," the local mover, Tom, said as he plopped box number thirty-seven on the ground, "I understand why y'all moved."

With the benefit of having lived in New York, I realized the New Yorkers were just being direct, not rude. In Tennessee, however, these two are sometimes synonymous, as Southerners tend to soften their language in many ways.

Take Arkansas native President Clinton (of it-depends-on-what-your-definition-of-"is"-is fame) as an example. He was known to utter sentences like "I might should do that," which suggests a greater sense of hesitance than just the word "should." This allows for a little wiggle room on both his part and the listeners'. The words "can," "may," and "must" modify main verbs to express possibility and probability, and Southerners just throw them all in a sentence at once. For instance, when I asked the movers nervously, "Do you think y'all could load back up some of the larger pieces of furniture and take them to a storage place down the road?" Tom said, "We might could."

Notice that he didn't say the definite "we could" or the less certain "we might." Rather, he used both "might" and "could" to form a phrase that roughly translates into "it's not out of the realm of possibility, but I'm not committing to anything."

The Southern use of multiple modals follows a few general rules—the first modal is "might" or "may," the second is usually "can," "could," "would," "should," "will," or "oughta." There's at least one triple modal commonly used in Southern speech—"might shouldoughta"—and "useta" sometimes precedes modals as well (for example, "I useta could fit all my furniture in my apartment.")[1] This gives Southerners a politeness strategy not possible in other regional dialects and allows for greater civility when the grammatically correct "should" seems too direct. Telling the mover "You should take my stuff to storage for me" would be rude, because it's too definite, like a demand. However, "You might could take that couch down to storage for me" sounds like a suggestion.

Even in confrontational mode, Southerners employ verbal mechanisms to take the edge off. Whereas the New York movers tell the others to "move it," the Tennesseans ask why they're "as slow as molasses in January."

By four o'clock, I still hadn't broached the storage space subject with Sarge. In addition to being afraid he'd say no, I realized I needed someone to watch the children. They were underfoot as it was, trying to watch a movie in the corner of the apartment, and I couldn't just leave them in the vehicle parked on the side of the road while I arranged the furniture storage. My aunt Mary was on her way from Nashville, so I figured I'd wait to bring it up till she was there to babysit.

"You don't have to say thank you and please *every time*," Mike told me, plopping the box down at my feet. "I'll be back here about a hundred times before we're done, and you're really just slowing down the process."

So the next time he came up and delivered a box of books for me, it took every ounce of self-control to force my lips to remain shut. It almost physically hurt me to say, "Put that in the office" without attaching a "please" and "thanks."

Tom was somewhat bemused at the exchange. "Now, it don't waste any time to say those short little words." I smiled but was beginning to doubt I could convince them to go to Store-All if they were interested in streamlining our *syllables*. "I don't know how you lived up there as long as you did," Tom said as he walked out the door.

In the South, we feel free to make conversation with anyone we find ourselves in contact with—even in the most uncomfortable situations. (I was in the doctor's office waiting room the other day when the woman next to me and I chatted amiably for half an hour—only to find out later that she was having a heart attack.) They'll even comment on *other people's* conversations if they're within earshot. In the city, everyone pretends not to hear people talking—even in the elevator—to give those in densely populated areas a little privacy.

Of course, the next time Mike came up, I instinctively said, "Thanks."

"Don't mention it." He rolled his eyes. "Really."

"Sorry."

"What're you apologizing for?" he said, annoyed. Mike obviously wanted to place a box at my feet, check off the number, and be given instructions where to move it. My conversational efforts to befriend him every time he made it to the top of the stairs were beginning to wear thin.

"Okay, sorry," I said. "Oops—sorry!"

I also apparently have a rare form of Tourette's syndrome that causes me to apologize instead of to curse. "I'm sorry" sometime means nothing more to Southerners than "Let's move on" or "I regret that happened to you." A Philly friend once looked at me funny when I said "I'm sorry" after she complained excessively about her kid wetting the bed and keeping her up all night.

"Why? Was it *your* fault he wet the bed?" she asked. In that case, of course, I'd really meant, "Look, lady, we all have problems. Just quit complaining already."

The fact of the matter is that people from different parts of America simply communicate differently, so it's quite possible to mistake friendliness for rudeness even between the closest of friends. Rene and I had to overcome this early in our relationship, as conversations with her often occurred with machine-gun rapidity. Take this exchange about a friend of ours transferring schools:

"I just heard Ella isn't sending her daughter to this school anymore, she's—"

"Get out!" she interrupted.

"That's what I heard. Apparently, she's transferring her to—"

"Where's she sending her?"

"A school closer to her house, at least that's what Jessic—"

"Where'd you hear this?"

"Jessica told me—even though she's vice pres—"

"Isn't she a PTA officer?"

"—ident. Maybe you should run."

At first her lively and enthusiastic responses sometimes shocked me into a stunned silence. I was brought up to allow a proper amount of time to pass after someone stops speaking to make sure he or she has completed the thought. To me, Rene's constant questioning felt more like a hostile interrogation instead of a casual conversation. If I made a good point in a discussion, she approved quickly and loudly. But if she didn't agree with me (which happened with alarming frequency due to her good sense), she definitely let me know. I used to stop talking mid-story to allow her to talk, not realizing she was merely encouraging me to elaborate. For similar reasons, we also have difficulty talking on the telephone.

But Rene and I gradually worked through our conversational differences. She had to tell me, "When my voice sounds like *this*, it means I find what you're saying really interesting. When I nod vigorously, I'm not trying to hurry you up. I'm agreeing with you." Because conversational cues between us were sent, received, and processed without us even realizing what was happening, it would've been easy to think our friendship lacked chemistry when in reality, we just lacked a common manner of communication.

The New York and Tennessee movers were irritating one another due in part to these kinds of issues. Instead of thinking, *Sarge doesn't give me the customary half-second pause to make sure I've finished talking*, Tom just assumed he was pushy. Sarge apparently thought Southerners worked as slowly as they talked. Since Tennesseans typically elongate their words, stretching them out cordially, even a simple exchange of information sounds pleasant and amiable . . . and maybe a little slow. (This is, by the way, why Southern women have a much higher pregnancy rate than Northern women—because it takes them three times as long to say "Stop that!")

At 5:30, my aunt called. She was, of course, lost.

All four movers stood there straining under the weight of the boxes, waiting for me to check them off and direct them. "Box eleven," Sarge whispered, "and box eight."

"Can you just ask someone for directions?" I asked Aunt Mary. It was getting dark, and I knew she couldn't drive well at night. With each passing minute, the words of the Store-All cashier rang louder in my ears: "Be outta here by closing time. That electronic gate turns off every night at seven o'clock."

Over the next half hour, she called five more times, more lost than before. I tried my best to check off the boxes, to pacify the children, and to figure out directions . . . but the time approached 6:00, then 6:15. Finally, I took a deep breath and approached Sarge. Store-All was just a mile down the road, I thought. With four guys, we had plenty of time to get the furniture in the unit.

I cleared my throat. "Excuse me—"

"Maybe you can't read the word 'fragile'?" Sarge said to Tom, after he dropped a box on the floor with a clank.

"I *know* how to move a box," he said, his blood rushing to his face. Both the Tennesseans stiffened into motionless statues of indignation.

"Listen, I need to get outta here," Tom said. My hopes were fast dissipating. I had to get a sleeper sofa and a desk my dad had lovingly made me into storage. He'd bought a walnut tree from the Historical Society in 1973 from the property of Andrew Jackson, and had kept it for years before fashioning it into my desk. It was stunning, beautiful, and—like everything Daddy makes—built to withstand the Apocalypse. That desk was so large we couldn't have fit it into our 1,300-square-foot apartment without butter, a shoehorn, and a miracle. I watched Tom put down his box and take off his gloves; I'd waited just a few minutes too long. Well, we still had three workers, so the odds were with us. Three workers, one couch, one desk, and forty-five minutes.

"I've got to get going too," said the other local mover. "And if you're ever in Tennessee again, make sure you call and tell us so I'll be sure to make other plans."

Sarge handed the workers some cash and shook his head while he surveyed the amount of work that remained. "Sarge?" I began, my voice a little shaky at 6:21. "Do you think, I mean, would it be possible, if it wasn't inconvenient, for you to . . ."

I took a deep breath. He had a truck; I had some cash. . . . I didn't have the time to be hesitant. "Would you take my desk and sofa to a storage space about a mile away?"

Sarge glanced at his watch, then at the other worker. "That'll cost you," he said. He looked up at the ceiling, trying not to be annoyed. They'd been working several hours and didn't want to be working late into the night. "Okay," he said, as if he was convincing himself. We'd already asked him to move us from the apartment to our new farmhouse after it was built. Maybe he was trying to keep our future business when he blurted, "We'll do it."

I was so touched that they were so willing to accommodate me that I almost couldn't tell him the rest.

"The place closes at seven," I added.

All three of us looked at the clock. "And that means we need to be *out of* there by seven," I clarified, in a barely audible voice.

They activated—reloading the furniture they'd already unloaded from the truck. I grabbed the kids, buckled them in their car seats, and called Aunt Mary.

"You almost here?" I asked sweetly. I had no idea how I'd get the movers into the unit with the kids in tow. Her trip, which should've normally taken about thirty minutes, had taken her two hours. And she wasn't sure of her location.

By the time all of us got to the storage space (eighteen-wheelers move more slowly through traffic than snails on Valium), it was 6:46. The storage facility had ten long rows of units with orange garage-style doors, surrounded by a twelve-foot security fence with barbed wire coils. I jumped out of the vehicle, ran to the electronic gate—which had a little keypad—and fumbled with the receipt to find the gate code.

While Sarge and Mike unloaded the truck, I experienced that sinking feeling that usually accompanies extreme stupidity or bad fortune—like when you realize you've slept through the alarm. No matter how much I looked, I couldn't find the code to open the gate.

It was 6:49.

"What's wrong with you?" Sarge asked, seeing my pawing through my vehicle like a dog looking for a bone. I thrust the yellow paper at him, tears running down my face. "There's no code . . . on this . . . sheet," I sobbed. He grabbed the paper and immediately looked at me. I guess I was so anxious I couldn't even see the four large numbers written in black ink on the paper.

My relief was short-lived; the code didn't work. I tried, then Sarge tried. We stood in the dark for so long I wondered if we looked suspicious enough to catch the attention of police officers. As soon as the thought occurred to me, three sets of headlights rushed up and surrounded us in a semicircle, their brakes squealing to a stop. I couldn't see past the glaring lights, but visions of being dragged off in handcuffs with my New York movers flashed through my head. I was just about to break into "Nobody Knows the Trouble I've Seen" when I heard a voice come from one of the cars.

"These y'all's?" she asked, maneuvering around the sofa and desk.

The much maligned "y'all" is probably the most notorious feature of a Southerner's vocabulary, a probable contraction of "you" and "all," but I'd never been happier to hear it. This lady was definitely *not* a cop and had used the word's possessive form, which selfishly utilizes not one but *two* apostrophes—thumbing its nose at the draconian when-in-doubt, leave-it-out mantra we learned in grammar school. While in the North, I tried not to say "y'all"—not to hide my Southern identity, which was impossible, but to avoid having the conversation devolve into how "cute" my accent was. To compensate, I'd end up saying "you guys"—which sounded about as natural coming from my mouth as "thou." The fact is, English teachers throughout history have always demanded that "you" act as both a singular and a plural form. Philadelphians rebel against this ambiguity with irksome "youse" or "youse guys." Around Pittsburgh, people say "yunz" or "yinz," a contraction of "you ones."[2] Bostonians, however, have no need for a second person plural. They believe some people just aren't worth addressing and are never so indeterminate as to want to talk to *everyone* (while Southerners have the even more inclusive "all y'all").

The lady who'd driven up with two other cars had a familiar look of panic in her eyes, because she too was frantically trying to get inside the gate before closing. Seeing Sarge struggle with the keypad, she yelled, "Try my code—eleven twenty-six!"

I thanked her, and she yelled back, "No problem, but you better hurry—that gate won't budge after seven."

By the time I turned around, Sarge and Mike had the sofa on

one dolly and the desk on another. I locked the doors of the Land Rover, activated the vehicle's security alarm, and took off running down the long, dark corridor. I could hear Sarge and Mike pushing the rickety dollies behind me in our weird furniture relay—perhaps a feature *Extreme Home Makeover* could add to spice up their format. The numbers of the units were decreasing as we ran. Fifty-four, fifty-two, fifty, forty-eight . . .

"Where's the unit?" Sarge asked. I didn't want to admit yet that I didn't exactly know its location, so I kept running. And running. Finally we reached the end of the row which ended at thirty. And that was that. No more units, no more rows. I came to an abrupt stop and Sarge and Mike somehow kept the furniture from toppling on me.

I was out of breath, in a near panic, and my watch read 6:56. At the end of the row, in the shadows, I detected that there might be a path to another set of units.

Then, off in the distance, an alarm sounded.

Beep—beep—beep—beep—beep.

Someone was trying to open the doors of the Land Rover.

I tossed the keys to the elusive unit to Sarge and took off faster than Jackie Joyner-Kersee. What had possessed me to leave two precious children locked in a car on a dark side street? I normally wouldn't even do that to a dog. As I ran, I thought of all the things I'd say to them, all the love I'd shower on them, and all the apologies I'd make for leaving them locked in the car . . . if only they were safe.

As I approached, I made out the outlines of the kids in their car seats. Camille's door was ajar.

"I reeeeally have to go to the bathroom," she said, her head hanging out the open door. She had somehow managed to pull open the lock from inside, which set off the alarm. By this time, I had literally sweated through my clothes and smelled like a wrestler after a match (having left my deodorant in our Philly apartment three days ago).

It was 6:59. I ran back to the gate and realized with a sinking heart that Sarge and Mike were nowhere in sight. Slowly, the gate began to close. The thought occurred to me that maybe this gate worked like a grocery store door and would reopen if I threw my body in front of it. It, however, was no gentleman . . . relentlessly pushing me farther and farther as my feet dug into the asphalt.

In a sudden burst of inspiration, I ran back to the keypad. According to my watch, I still had thirty seconds. Maybe if the gate was open when the power was turned off, it'd stay open all night. Miraculously, I remembered the lady's code. When I punched in the last number, the gate stopped, and started to reluctantly rise.

Suddenly, I saw two tiny dots in the darkness coming toward me in the corridor. Evidently, Sarge and Mike had found my unit, locked up the furniture, and were making a mad dash of escape. The gate had just completely gotten open and was beginning to eke its way down in the opposite direction.

"Run!" I yelled. "You can beat it!"

In a demonstration of athleticism not seen in the first half of our furniture relay, they sprinted toward me, the dollies clanking behind in protest. At the last possible moment, they darted through and the gate shut decisively behind them. They immediately bent over at their waists, panting, like runners on the other side of a finish line, although there were no people handing out cups of water or medals.

"I'll make this up to you in your tips," I said, thankful for their near-heroic efforts.

"When we move you out to the farm," Sarge began, "could you try to have things a little more organized?"

I thought about the logistics of moving an eighteen-wheeler to a home in a heavily wooded location currently accessible only by four-wheelers, about my countless broken New Year's resolutions to get my life together, and about how good workers like Sarge help me get things done in spite of my thoughtlessness.

Even though he was from New York, I think he saw right through me when I smiled at him and responded, in all sincerity, "I might could."

Shopping and Other
Noncompetitive Activities

"IT'S JUST EXERCISE," Rene told me as we walked out the door, leaving our children in a suspiciously serene yoga studio with low square seats in the corners and soothing colors on the walls. "And a way to have noncompetitive fun." I'd never done yoga and suspected the South Street studio was a cover for getting the children to "bow to the sun god" or support future Green Party candidates. Nevertheless, I let the children participate in a few sessions and found myself standing outside the studio with an hour to kill.

"Come shopping with us," Rene offered as she and her friend headed off to the large organic food supermarket. This had become their routine, since the yoga instructor locked the class doors so parents wouldn't disturb the tranquillity of their "space." (Maintaining one's space is, I noticed, of utmost importance in cities—whether it be the personal three feet surrounding an individual or his area otherwise known as apartment 2B.)

"I still don't get why we can't stay and wait," I said to Rene.

"It has to do with maintaining a constant flow of good energy," she explained.

I shuffled my feet and allowed myself to be prodded along to the supermarket. But when we stepped into the store, I was amazed. I wasn't prepared for the endless array of fresh foods and meat that awaited us. I'd never eaten an olive, and had definitely never seen an olive bar. I'd never tasted fresh peanut butter and had certainly never ground the nuts myself. I bought whole chocolate milk in a glass bottle, an unidentifiable substance called couscous, and an herbal antiperspirant that made me smell like I'd run a marathon in a wool suit—all for the price of a midsize sedan.

I'd tried to shop at this store before but had been thwarted by the parking garage when alarms went off and lights flashed—Evil SUV Alert! Evil SUV Alert!—evidently because it lacked enough clearance to accommodate such a vehicle. One store across town had a convenient outdoor parking lot but prohibited the grocery carts from leaving the store. This left me in the uncomfortable position one day when I had to decide whether I should leave the groceries next to the homeless guy asking for a dollar, leave the kids to protect the food while I ran for the car, or ask the kids to follow me to and from the cart about thirty times and hope the guy stole slowly.

My only real choice was to leave the food, buckle the kids into the vehicle, lock the doors, and sprint back across the parking lot. By the time I'd done that, the man had already taken two bags of food from my cart.

"What are you doing?" I asked.

He didn't move.

"Put the bags down," I said calmly. Of course he immediately slid both bags onto his left arm, so he could freely rummage through the remaining merchandise. I suspected he was pulling a Ronald Reagan—using situational deafness to determine what he wanted to hear—because after he gathered up a few more sacks, he looked at me blankly and motioned to my vehicle.

Only then did I realize he wasn't holding my food hostage or planning to make himself a ham on rye. He actually possessed enough gall to be hustling for a tip by "helping" with my groceries against my will. As he held my melting ice cream in his grimy hands, I thought of all the clean-cut Southern young men who used to carry my items from the checkout counter to my trunk, politely inquiring about my day and refusing all tips.

Those Southern grocery store employees also kindly offered assistance inside the store, helping me find exotic products like ramen noodles and Spam. Not that you have to find things quickly in a Southern grocery store. Their aisles are wide enough to browse, compare prices, and taste the meatball on a toothpick the hairnetted ladies offer passersby. (I had friends in college who fulfilled 100 percent of their nutritional needs with the freebies in the Green Hills Kroger in Nashville.)

In cities, however, limited space dictates that grocery store lanes are so narrow Nicole Richie and Paris Hilton couldn't fit in one simultaneously. Shopping there is like being on a conveyor belt: you're unable to stop the momentum of the cart because the invisible social pressure exerted by the person behind you propels you forward. Not possessing the natural brazenness to compete for floor space, I tried to memorize the precise location of all our favorite products. (Sometimes we'd have toilet paper, and sometimes we'd just hope I could grab it next time.) Frequently, however, I couldn't even locate these.

"Yes, we have Coca-Cola," the New York cashier told me one day, after I failed to find what I thought was a basic human necessity. "But they're in the back. There's no shelf space, so we leave them back there until you buy these," he said, pointing to a whole row of Fresca. This was the cold reality of not having space. So we bought Honeycombs instead of Mini-Wheats, whole milk instead of skim, and sweet pickles instead of mouthwash, hoping we wouldn't miss the day that our favorite items made a fleeting appearance on the shelf.

Making it even worse, the cashier had a keen eye. Every single Monday I stood across from him while he compared the signature on the receipt with the signature on my credit card.

"This doesn't match," he'd say, sliding the receipt back over and keeping my Visa.

And he'd always be right. My mood largely dictates what my signature looks like, and I have many options to choose from. First, I have the upper-left-hand-corner-of-my-homework signature I used almost exclusively in the fourth grade. Then there's the I-don't-want-the-person-behind-me-to-wait-any-longer scrawl on the bottom of checks. And of course I've perfected the optimistic and important-looking I'll-use-this-when-I'm-famous illegible scribble.

The problem begins when I'm at home opening the mail at the kitchen table. There, I use a Sharpie on the back of my newly arrived credit card and take the time to form the letters artfully, each loop in hopeful anticipation of future purchases. But when I'm actually buying the items, I invariably rush, and sometimes (or in New York, every Monday) the cashier raises an eyebrow.

"Try again," he said, handing me the pen but withholding the card for verification. You'd think this would be a simple case of writing more neatly, but with several credit cards (all with different-looking names on the back) and hundreds of possible signatures, I'd sweat it every time.

In other words, I was never what you'd call a savvy urban shopper. This was never more obvious than when I decided— after one too many brushes with homeless men, parking garages, and cart restrictions—to quit driving to the store. This is not a revolutionary concept in the city, as people use handy little carts to transport their goods home. I, however, didn't have one, so I used the next best thing—an umbrella stroller. After all, it was only seven blocks and we were just picking up a few things.

Grocery needs, of course, multiply like loaves or fish. By the time we got to the register that afternoon, we'd spent $167. I saw a small bead of sweat form on David's brow, but I smiled smugly and unfolded my secret weapon: the light blue Mickey Mouse stroller we'd bought at Sears. Finally I'd been responsible enough to plan ahead. I thought triumphantly, I'll use the stroller, David will admire my attributes as a wife, and we'll have fresh Frosted Flakes in the morning.

I was admittedly a little surprised when the stroller swayed dramatically under the heft of a single gallon of milk. I loaded it up nonetheless and put on the happy countenance of one who regularly takes her bacon and cheese out for a walk. We struggled through seven blocks, fighting to keep the stroller upright and the tautly hung bags from amputating our arms. By the time we got into our building, the eggs were broken, our arms were striped red with indentations from the bags, and the bread was as flat as Al Gore's personality. When we finally made it to the door of our apartment, the stroller—in one last burst of protest before collapsing—popped off one of its wheels, which rolled all the way down the hall in an almost cinematic gesture.

Compared to my typical grocery misadventures, in other words, strolling through Whole Foods with Rene during the kids' yoga class was actually quite pleasant . . . although I was still a little annoyed the instructor wouldn't let the parents wait in the studio.

"She doesn't want to mess up the studio's spiritual harmony," Rene explained for the thousandth time.

"That's ridiculous," I said.

"It's just a fact," she said. "Some people unknowingly bring in bad energy, ya know? You don't want people who are frazzled and harried by the details of life to be hanging around."

"You're right," I conceded as we walked up the stairs and waited for the door to be unlocked for us. "I don't want *those* kinds of people around my children."

Eatin' Good in the Neighborhood

"YOU'RE A GOOD cook, aren't you?"

We'd been attending Tenth Presbyterian Church in Philadelphia for months and still had yet to develop friendships with any other members. So when the people sitting in front of us one Sunday—Bill and Marguerite—invited us to lunch, we hoped our instant and breathless yes didn't come off as too desperate. Conversation about jobs and church went well—until they asked us to visit their exclusive gourmet club comprised of their close, food-loving friends from college.

I wasn't about to ruin my chances by telling her my idea of an hors d'oeuvre was squirty cheese on a Ritz. I'd always heard that if you can read, you can cook. And if it was just a matter of following directions, then I figured, "Of course I can cook." The words escaped my mouth and David somehow managed not to injure himself when he fell on the floor laughing hysterically.

The theme of our debut month was Mexican—and I was told in advance I'd be bringing nachos and guacamole.

"Guacamole?" Rene asked incredulously. "Are you sure you're supposed to bring that to a *gourmet* dinner?"

No, actually, I wasn't sure, because David had lost the faxed recipe on the way home from work. After frantic calls to the hostess went unreturned, I wondered what kind of people fax recipes anyway? Were they stuck in the 1990s? Did they have answering machines with microtapes instead of voice mail, VHS players perpetually blinking 12:00 instead of a DVD player? I bet they'd never even heard of TiVo or e-mail.

Rene is a great Jewish cook and wanted me to make Christian friends in Philadelphia—partly because she realized the importance of spiritual community to me and partly because she was sick of listening to me talk about Jesus. So she gave me a list of groceries and offered to help me prepare the dish at her home that Saturday.

"I have no idea which cheeses are native to Latin America," I said, looking at my list, exasperated.

"Now, just calm down, Nancy. Are you cooking Mexi*can*, or Mexi*can't*?"

My rising irritation was compounded by protesters outside the grocery store holding placards with Dick Cheney's photo scrawled with the question "The Antichrist?" The store was located on Philadelphia's most notorious street, South Street, which has bars, tattoo parlors, sexual toy shops, vagrants, homemade band advertisements adhered to lightposts with used chewing gum, and political activists. During the election, I had somehow managed to tolerate the protesters that lurked outside stores. But now, many months after Bush had won, I was beginning to wonder if I'd ever get any nonpartisan grocery shopping done. When they solicited me, I told them—for fun—"I actually support Social Security privatization."

"What's all that booing?" Rene said over the phone.

"Forget that," I said. "You've got to help me find this food."
I had never bought authentic Mexican queso fresco, cilantro,
and black beans, but I definitely knew they weren't located in
the SpaghettiO aisle. Rene knew this place as well as her own
kitchen, so I walked into the store with the phone pressed to my
ear as she gave me step-by-step instructions.

"Okay, now take about ten steps forward and look to your
right."

"I don't see them," I said.

"The avocados should be on your right. Look down a little."

I glanced nervously around at the boxes of beautiful, strange
foods, trying desperately to find the last and most critical ingredient. "All I see are these weird-shaped black things."

"Nancy, what do you think an avocado looks like?" Obviously, I had no idea. I'd never eaten one, I'd never purchased
one, and I definitely couldn't pick one out of a police lineup.
"Are you trying to tell me they're *black*?" The customers around
started to snicker, but I wasn't ashamed. I mean, the peel of a banana is yellow, the skin of an orange is orange, so logic would
dictate that the outside of an avocado would be light green, no?

After an hour, I lumbered past the protesters, carrying my
grain-fed beef and my organic lettuce, and they booed and hissed
at me until I finally got to my vehicle. I have never been happier to own a gas-guzzling Land Rover, and I only wished I had
a bumper sticker that read "I Don't Brake for Pacifists." Next
time.

I showed up at Rene's disheveled and reeling from the im-
possibility of the culinary task before me. She and her mother

(herself a gourmet cook, visiting from Florida) dug immediately into the groceries and went to work, teaching me as they went along. I paid attention to every detail and occasionally stirred the pot or salted the emerging green blob (the technical, culinary term) so that I could honestly say I helped in the preparation. It's not that I don't enjoy food, quite the contrary. It's just that I grew up with much simpler tastes—chicken fried in Crisco. I can't tell you what cumin tastes like or why porcini mushrooms are so expensive. But by the time I arrived at the gourmet club, I was ready to pull off the hoax.

"This guacamole is exquisite," someone said. "Did you use lemon or lime juice?"

I was standing in front of rows of cookbooks and food magazines that made Martha Stewart's library look understocked. Without hesitation, I answered, "Lime, of course. I thought lemon would've been too pungent."

Over the course of the next three hours, David and I were silently evaluated by everyone in the group; their unwritten policy was that new members had to be unanimously approved. The men regaled me with stories about cooking with famous chefs, and the women spoke dreamy eyed of the perfect ganache. I nodded knowingly, hoping ganache was not an ingredient I was supposed to have included in my guacamole.

Thankfully, the conversation was not all about food. When they asked about my education I phrased my answers carefully.

"I went to NYU," I said. "Majored in philosophy." I'd learned long ago if I worded it like that, people would just assume I'd *graduated* from NYU with a *degree* in philosophy. To my horror, several of them had studied philosophy too, and started asking my opinion on Nietzsche's nihilism. Thankfully, the host pulled out the Style section of the *New York Times* to show off a photo of him with his arm around Salman Rushdie. "Oh, it was nothing. . . . Salman and I had just gotten some sort of humanitarian award," he demurred.

I didn't know if I could keep up my culinary charade if I had to feign being interesting too. These people were smart, articulate, and well educated. However, in spite of all their advanced degrees in various fields, their main passion was cooking . . . and therein was the problem.

By the time dessert and carefully selected dessert wines were served, I knew we were in over our heads. I thanked the host, gathered up Rene's Tupperware, and tried to slither out of the house unnoticed.

To my utter surprise, Bill came up to David and whispered, "Listen, I've been talking to everyone here, and we all think you and Nancy would be a great addition to our group."

Operation Gourmet Ruse was a success.

Like clockwork, I showed up every two months at Rene's with a faxed recipe and a bag of groceries. But the deception grew more and more difficult to sustain, as the recipes they faxed me increased in complexity. Once the hostess called me with my culinary assignment: "This month, I'm making braised lamb. You make the jasmine rice pilaf to go under it and the pomegranate sauce to go over it. Sound good?"

"Delicious," I said, though the sauce's main ingredient sounded like a countertop.

"You have to make the rice six hours in advance, but you might want to just throw the sauce together once you get here so it'll be fresh." I agreed that only the freshest pomegranate sauce would do, hung up the phone, and called Rene in a state of near panic.

"They're onto me!" I yelled.

"It'll be fine," Rene assured me. "I'll prepare everything here in little baggies, and all you have to do is sauté the onions when you arrive."

"I don't sauté, Rene," I said, exasperated. "Don't you know that by now?"

"Calm down; that just means you put it in a skillet and fry it."

"Can't I just bring my Fry Daddy?"

As if that wasn't bad enough, I learned that every member of the group took turns hosting a dinner at their respective homes. When it was my turn to host, Rene agreed to bail me out of certain disaster, coming over and pretending to be my housekeeper.

My friendship with Rene had grown one dish at a time over the course of the gourmet racket. She had taught me how to prepare traditional Jewish dishes (like beef brisket) and not-so-traditional Jewish meals. Since we lived near Chinatown with easy access to seaweed paper, bamboo mats called *sushimaki sudare*, and fresh fish, she even taught me how to make my own sushi.

"Okay, roll it up just like you'd roll a joint," she told me after we put the fish on the sticky rice.

"Um, I'm afraid you're going to have to be more specific than that."

No matter how little I knew about food, Rene always was

there with instruction and encouragement. After one particularly tough gourmet assignment, I wiped my hands on my apron and asked, "Do you think I should just give up and go back to Cracker-Barrel land?"

"What's cracker barrel?" she asked.

"Half store, half down-home cooking," I explained, aghast she'd never even seen the restaurant that's been called "Red America condensed into chain-restaurant form."[1] "They're everywhere."

"Oh, the *franchise*," Rene said with a smirk. "I went there once. They didn't serve bagels, and I never went back."

"You're such a food snob," I said.

"I just don't eat at *franchises*," she declared as if the word "franchise" meant maggot-infested salad bar.

"None of them?"

"Not purposefully."

"What about Waffle House?"

"You mean Awful Waffle?"

"Olive Garden?"

"The worst experience of my adult life."

"Chi-Chi's?"

"Of course not."

"Shoney's?"

"No, although it *is* owned by a Jew."

"McDonald's?"

"I find anyone who'd eat a McRibs or a Filet-O-Fish suspicious."

In fact, when John Kerry lost the 2004 election to George Bush, political adviser Doug Sosnik believed he knew why: Applebee's. "Our leaders—particularly Washington, D.C. based—don't really have the same life, day to day, as all those people out there in those red states. We don't eat at the same restaurants. I don't know many politicians in town that are leaders of our party who voluntarily go to Applebee's."[2] Sosnik continued, "We can't figure out a better way to sell to those people—we've got to be more like them."

I grew up thinking only upper-crust Americans got to eat at places like that—I used to drive two hours for the privilege of eating at the nearest one in Clarksville, Tennessee. And when Rene heard I ate at Shoney's on prom night—and was thrilled to be there—she was so disturbed she almost couldn't make my guacamole.

There's just something about a good "fern bar" that blue staters cannot comprehend. The service is usually friendly, the food is predictably good, and the price doesn't require portable defibrillators. Some chains even have curbside takeout, so diners can get food without the extra exertion of turning off the ignition. Soon, Ruby Tuesday will sell liquefied burgers administered intravenously.

In the aftermath of Sosnik's comments, pundits had a field day. Michael Graham wrote a farcical letter from an Applebee's manager to the Democratic Party leaders answering their purported questions.[3] They included the following clarifications:

- Applebee's is a neighborhood restaurant that encourages folks to enjoy food, fun, and friends! Reservations are not accepted or required.

- While we encourage healthy dining . . . we do not offer a vegan menu at this time. We apologize for the inconvenience.
- We would like to discourage you from asking [our servers] personal questions about the following: church attendance, gay marriage, abortion rights, their political affiliations, and whether or not they think President Bush is a "spoiled rich kid who wouldn't [urinate] on them if they were on fire."
- Neither Applebee's, Applebee's International, or the Blue Ridge Mall of Kansas City are owned by Halliburton or any of its subsidiaries.
- As a neighborhood bar and grill, we try to create a climate of camaraderie among our customers. . . . We are not, however, able to honor requests to seat your party (as one e-mail put it) "in the redneck section."
- While we have no doubt that the '94 Châteauneuf du Pape is a "scrappy little red with a crisp bouquet and a saucy hint of berries," we will not be adding it to our wine list at this time. Might we suggest a Bud Light?
- If you ask a fellow patron to show you his guns, please be advised that firearms are not allowed in the mall or the restaurant. You'll have to go out to his truck.

Graham's column was trying to demonstrate what anyone with common sense knows—that people who won't eat at Applebee's obviously don't love America. Well, they might love it but want to turn it into a croissant-eating, clove cigarette-smoking, Subaru-driving, Birkenstock-wearing, Bill Maher–watching, Camus-reading, terrorist-accommodating wasteland where you have to pay $17 for a glass of Sutter Home.

But you can't really blame the food snobs; you gotta blame their parents. I learned a long time ago at a mommy-and-me music class in Ithaca that the aversion to normal American cuisine is established at a young age. One morning, we sat on our carpet square and sang a song called "In the Kitchen," in which the peppy song leader encouraged the children to share what they had for breakfast.

"Let's go to the kitchen on our feet. What kind of breakfast did Hannah eat?"

"A bagel!" said Hannah, thrilled at the attention as her mother beamed proudly.

"Let's go to the kitchen on our feet. What kind of breakfast did Luke eat?"

"Quiche!" said Luke, rubbing his tummy. His father laughed good-naturedly.

"Let's go to the kitchen on our feet. What kind of breakfast did Camille eat?"

"Grits!" said Camille, happy to be called on.

"Pardon?"

"Grits," I enunciated.

"What's a *frit*?"

"A grit. G-rit. Grits, actually. Nobody can eat just one. They're . . . well. It looks like mushed-up rice."

"Like quinoa?"

"Like corn."

"Like tabouli?"

So, actually, I think we can all see that it's not the fault of the food snobs or their parents but rather the collective fault of all Northeastern music instructors. If they chose less polarizing songs (traditional classics like "If You're Happy and You Know It" or "I'm a Little Teapot"), then the organic Cheerios–eating electorate might just grow up with more tolerance in their hearts toward the Lucky Charms constituency—and America would be a much friendlier place to eat.

What Can Brown Do for You?

THE MOST EXPENSIVE meal I ever cooked was two hot dogs and a handful of French fries one day when we lived in Kentucky. After pouring some peanut oil in the skillet to heat, I set its large container near the stove while I prepared the potatoes. Camille was watching television in an adjacent room, and Austin was taking an uncharacteristic nap in the back of the house.

Suddenly I heard a loud clang followed by a yell, and all the shreds of common sense I possessed vanished. I left the stove, ran down the hall to his little room, and found him sitting on the floor. His truck blanket was curled around his feet, and he was crying large tears. I scooped him up to comfort him. Although David claims I also read *War and Peace*, made fruit baskets for the elderly, painted my fingernails, and then watched them dry, the truth is that I came right back to the kitchen . . . although perhaps I didn't exactly hurry. I'd already stopped thinking about the stove and was trying to figure out how to get Austin used to sleeping in a bed without rails. By the time I returned to the kitchen, Camille was standing on a chair screaming at the sight of a towering flame dancing from the stove.

David's New York law firm used to represent the manufac-
turer of Crisco. I vividly recall how shaken he was over cases
where people—in spite of the instructions on the label—had left
the stove unattended and then tried to fight the resulting grease
fire with water. I never forgot his descriptions of their injuries
and their damaged lives, and how sad he felt having to defend
the company against people whose lives were forever ruined by
the mistake of not heeding the warning on the label. So when I
saw the fire, I made a conscious decision not to reach for the
faucet. After that, I acted on sheer instinct. I ran the kids next
door, called 911, and did what every fireman warns against—I
went back into the house to fight the fire myself. After all, I
wasn't prepared to lose everything over a pot of fried potatoes.

At the time, we had a pretty substantial Amazon.com habit,
and it just so happened that a UPS man was delivering a package to me when he noticed the smoke coming out of the house
and a maniacal pajama-clad woman running into it. Without a
word or regard for his own safety, he ran in after me ("What can
Brown do for you?"), but we both came to an abrupt stop in the
dining room. Side by side we watched as my microwave melted,
fell onto the stove, and splattered drops of burning grease all
over the hardwood floors. My floor looked like the aerial view of
a concert with hundreds of cigarette lighters flickering to the
beat of the music.

I hadn't been able to reach our fire extinguisher (mainly because it was sitting in our old kitchen in upstate New York), and
the cabinets that held our flour were aflame. That's when the UPS
man turned and said his first words to me since he'd arrived on the
scene. "Ma'am, I think you've just burned your house down."

He was only partially right. The firemen easily extinguished the fire, but more than $30,000 of damage was already done. The hardwood floors, the carpets, all the appliances and countertops had to be replaced. Our clothes reeked so badly of smoke I ran up a four-digit dry-cleaning bill. We had to paint almost every wall in the house with three coats of paint. After six months of living with my in-laws, we were able to move back into our home. But from that moment on, whenever the kids saw emergency vehicles rushing to the scene of an accident, they'd pray. "Please, God, help whoever's in trouble." They had a keen awareness of how much was really at stake.

My kids have always been sensitive. Once, when I picked up my daughter from her Kentucky preschool, I was shocked to see tears rolling down her cheeks. Even though she was only four at the time, we called her the human tape recorder, as she could tell us with precision the details of her day—a characteristic that made her better than a nanny cam for evaluating new babysitters. When we got into the vehicle, she began telling me about her preschool lesson that day. It was called "Don't Talk to Strangers," but as she talked, I realized it more accurately could've been called "Don't Talk to Strangers or You Might Get Beheaded." Evidently the teacher had told the children true stories about kidnapping victims in an effort to scare them into not talking to strangers. Camille, whose idea of violence is when her brother's G.I. Joes attack her dolls, rattled on and on about children who were decapitated, thrown into lakes, and dismembered. Some kids cavalier enough to talk to strangers suffered atrocities that the teacher, with uncharacteristic discretion, couldn't even mention.

After she asked me exactly how heads could be torn off and what corpses were, I knew that many sleepless nights were in store for us. I expressed concern over the curriculum to the principal of the school, asking her if the next session, "Obey Police Officers," would be accompanied by videotapes of electric chair executions or if "Eat Vegetables" would feature photos of gastric bypass surgeries. In fact, Camille told us that a man had come into the class and offered the students candy. When some of the kids accepted it, the teacher revealed that the man was a "stranger" and said that the kids were lucky this wasn't the "real world," or they could've been one of the dead bodies floating in the lake.

After this, Camille began acting odd in public. At Wal-Mart, she cowered behind me, hiding from the elderly men in blue vests who handed out smiley-face stickers to customers at the door. Then in the checkout line, when the cashier smiled at the kids, I had to stifle Camille's screams for the police.

This scenario initiated many conversations among the parents about what exactly should be taught to the kids about strangers. While we all agreed that graphic descriptions of decapitation were not age appropriate, we also began questioning the very idea of "not talking to strangers." Since the children were young—and never without supervision—we didn't want to breed suspicion of adults at such an early age. After all, Southerners telling kids not to talk to people they didn't know was like ducks telling ducklings to stay away from water—there's just something incongruous about it. One parent said, referring to the parable of the Good Samaritan, "Doesn't the Bible tell us to talk to strangers?" We all looked at her blankly, as if the surgeon general had just announced that cigarette smoking helps reduce tooth decay. However, she had a point.

Something about the Southern culture—perhaps the way we're taught to look people in the eye and offer a firm hand-shake—makes people more congenial, more aware of each other's presence. For example, the simple tradition of opening doors for ladies causes people to be more cognizant of each other. Women move out of the way slightly, men quickly position themselves to open it unobtrusively, and women say a simple thank you as they pass through the portal—be it the door to the 7-Eleven or the entrance to church. Because it's a delicate dance of etiquette that requires the participation of both genders, Southern gentlemen sometimes look awkward in the North—falling all over themselves trying to open doors for urban women who don't expect the gesture.

In the South, if you brush up against someone in a bar, on the street, or in a diner, you stop, turn to the person inadvertently hit, put your hand on his or her shoulder or back, and apologize with a quick pat and a smile. It's not long and drawn out but a casual demonstration of goodwill and manners, a two-second courtesy to acknowledge someone's existence. When I moved to Manhattan, I was appalled at the way people bumped, jostled, and brushed up against me on the sidewalk without a single glance back. One of my first days there, I was jarred from behind—without apology, of course—and I was truly raring for a fistfight with this Wall Street jerk. As far as I was concerned, knocking people around like that is more aggressive than giving the middle finger, so I instinctively prepared for the worst. But what I saw surprised me—just the back of the man's suit as he rushed to the office. He had no ill will toward me; he just thought another pedestrian deserved about as much deference as a light pole.

In the South, depending on how crowded the sidewalk is, you smile, nod, and sometimes even say hello. You never have to overcome some sort of social stigma to ask for help. I remember riding in the backseat of our 1977 Mercury Marquis—a yellow-and-rust–colored car with brown velour seats, an eight-track that played only "Rocky Top," and one headlight that always stayed closed—on the way to the grocery store, when we stopped at a red light. A man who'd pulled up beside us rolled down his window and asked Daddy for directions to a certain place right outside town. Daddy tried his best to simplify the directions into a quick, memorable sound bite, but the light turned green and the man was apparently too lost to understand. Daddy yelled out his window, "Follow me!" We made a U-turn and led him all the way out of town to his destination, a twenty-minute detour.

That's just how Southerners operate, going the extra mile for anyone who needs it. A year after our house fire, however, we moved to Philadelphia, where our apartment was situated between three major hospitals, and shrieking ambulance sirens pierced the night constantly. At first I thought it was cute that the kids prayed at every siren, and I congratulated myself for raising compassionate kids. But in Philly, it seemed every five minutes we had moments of silence for random strangers in peril. "Dear God, please save whoever had to call nine-one-one and make them not be afraid," Austin would pray, his eyes wide open in alarm. On the street, in the park, even in bed, the ubiquitous sirens transformed kids normally absorbed with coloring books into virtual priests.

As time went by, I began rushing them through the tenth prayer of the day—which sometimes occurred before they ate their Froot Loops. Eventually they got the unspoken message that their desire for the welfare of others was sweet but inconvenient. Invariably, the sirens became just a part of our urban soundtrack, along with construction worker come-ons, honking horns, and the melodic sounds of jackhammers.

The longer we stayed in the city, the more callous I became. I began to put more and more distance between myself and others to ensure our own survival—both financial and emotional. I learned not to make eye contact on the street, give money to beggars, or make small talk on the bus. Eventually my daughter stopped asking why people lay on the subway grates with damp newspapers over their heads. Twice, I even watched the horrors of the late local news and managed to fall asleep afterward.

But when a woman was shot execution style in front of my building at 4:30 one morning, my protective emotional buffer was obliterated. With the details of the murder swirling in my mind, I walked home from a movie the following night. The murder victim had worked at a nearby hospital, lived in the suburbs; she had been followed off the bus and shot in the head while my family slept just yards away. It just so happened that the entire murder was caught on film. The grainy footage showed the perpetrator shooting her in the head without a word. He hadn't been caught yet, but police speculated (it turned out correctly) that he was a serial killer and warned Philadelphians he might strike again. I was alone that evening and tried to casually fall into step with a group of Chinese tourists, hoping I could hide in the safety of their numbers.

They, however, were lost. Since it would've seemed odd for me to hang out shuffling my feet as they consulted their map, I turned in front of the Liberty Bell. After all, the killer had already offed someone under the heavy surveillance of the historic area and was probably not going to come back to be filmed for a sequel. In fact, the police standing guard were whistling a cheery song as I passed. But as much as I tried to feel comfort in their nonchalance, I exhaled deeply and weighed the pros and cons of handgun ownership. City streets offered no eye contact, no friendly greetings, no UPS men who rescued damsels in distress.

It's not like mere congeniality would've saved the lady's life— she had been traveling alone on the street in the middle of the night, just as I was. As I shuffled down the street, I began to panic. I wanted desperately to join the other groups of people who were spread out over the streets, but language disparities and social customs made it impossible. If I'd said, "May I walk with you because I'm afraid?" the people would've thought I was crazy. Had I been in the South, the men would've insisted on escorting me, not just as far as our mutual paths ran together but until I made it safely to my door. My heart beat as quickly as if I'd been sprinting home, and I couldn't shake the feeling that this urban numbness made us all more susceptible to becoming victims.

Come to think of it, I can't remember the last time the kids prayed for a stranger. And honestly I don't even recall hearing the sirens during the early morning that woman was killed. However, I'm certain if I had, the only emotion I would have felt would have been annoyance over lost sleep.

But I feel we've lost a lot more.

EvilWhiteSoutherner

OUR FIRST WEEK in Philadelphia, I ill-fatedly walked my children by a man on the street who was loudly proclaiming white people were evil. He stood on a makeshift wooden platform, used a loudspeaker system, and was dressed in white robes. Several men stood around him, dressed similarly, their arms folded and their feet wide apart in a stance intended to intimidate. With all the noise of the Philadelphia streets, I didn't notice them until I was too close, so I told the kids to cover their ears as we rushed by. I'd encountered this group twice before in New York, once when the speaker called my shocked sister Amy a "she-devil" and another time in Union Square, when the speaker harshly pointed out my immodest clothing (jeans, a long-sleeved shirt, and a jacket), held me morally responsible for slavery, and told the crowd I deserved to be raped.

I lowered my eyes as we walked by, disturbed by the large audience he'd amassed, and thought we'd averted disaster until Camille looked up at me with wide eyes and asked, "White people are *devils?*" Those five-year-old chubby hands weren't as soundproof as I'd hoped.

"Some black people don't like white people because they're white, and some white people don't like black people because they're black," I said, trying my best to condense a complicated issue into understandable sound bites. "God tells us to love people no matter what their color is."

My smugness about handling that complex problem quite well, thank you, dissipated at the park later that day. We were at Seger Park in Philadelphia, which reminded me of those *Sesame Street* cement parks surrounded by iron gates and tall buildings. I watched both kids play catch with children of various colors and was happy they'd never know or understand the segregation of races. Camille was swinging next to her new friend, who wore her hair in a short Afro, while the girl's mother stood behind them and pushed their little bottoms. Austin and I approached just in time to hear Camille tell the mother, "I like your daughter even though she's black."

The urban warm fuzzies vanished, replaced by the cold realization that nothing I said could take the sting away from her comment. I must have had a look of sheer terror on my face, because Camille quickly added, "I mean, even though she's . . . khaki."

The South hadn't provided many opportunities for her to figure out the nuances of race relations, and I'd hoped Center City Philadelphia would be her classroom on diversity and tolerance. That day in the park, we had a crash course.

"Please avoid all conversations about skin color," I told my confused daughter, whose cheeks had turned crimson as I gently pulled her to the sidewalk.

A month later, when my new friend Jacqueline invited me

to see her Afro before she went to the salon, I was perplexed. Every other time I'd seen her, she'd had long, gorgeous hair. I had no idea how that could miraculously metamorphose into an Afro. "I've been wearing a wig," she said, laughing. "Don't you know anything about black women's hair?"

The answer was a definitive no.

I was further confused when she invited me to her playgroup in West Philadelphia called Mocha Moms.

"*Mocha* as in African American?" I asked her, trying to hide the distress in my voice. I'd like to report I pushed aside my apprehensions and expanded my racial horizons . . . that by the end of the playgroup we were swapping recipes and singing "We Are the World." But instead I politely declined.

"Why are you so hesitant?" she pressed, eyes narrowing as I avoided giving her a direct answer for over a week. Finally one day she pinned me down. "Are you going or not?"

"The truth of the matter is," I began, failing to come up with a believable excuse and resorting to the truth, "I'm not black."

She assured me Mocha Moms had a racial nondiscrimination policy, which was good to hear, but I was still a little uncomfortable. I mean, they didn't name it *Mocha* Moms to attract displaced white Southern women.

She drove me to the playgroup and didn't roll her eyes when I asked who was on the radio. ("It's Luther," she said, before registering my blank face and adding "Vandross.") We drove to West Philadelphia—"the hood," as she called it—and entered a community center with pictures of famous black leaders on the walls. Although we were the first ones there, the room quickly filled with attractive, educated, fashionable women who welcomed me warmly and never mentioned my lack of pigmentation. I don't remember ever being the only Caucasian in a room before.

"How'd you feel?" Jacqueline asked on the drive home.

"A little awkward," I admitted. "I felt I should address the fact that my skin isn't mocha, but I didn't want to Johnnie Cochran it up."

"Meaning . . ."

"You know, make race more of an issue than it should be."

She looked away from the road for a moment to glance at me. "You think O.J. was guilty?"

Jacqueline was the first person I'd met who actually believed O.J. was innocent. In fact, I'd thought the one thing all Americans could agree on was that he was not. That and never to purchase extended warranties from CompUSA. Suddenly I felt guilty of some sort of hate crime and mumbled something about not following the trial closely enough.

In other words, I was as confused as Camille that day at the park. In fact, even writing this chapter was an internal tug-of-war, as I continually modified words and edited language to be as innocuous as possible.

"You shouldn't use 'black' so much," my husband advised after reading it.

"Jacqueline says 'black,'" I mumbled, hitting delete and sprinkling in a few "African Americans" for good measure. As Camille pointed out, the terms "black" and "white" are not quite accurate enough, but "African American" is a little culturally insensitive—lumping all people of color into one continental generalization. It's ambiguous since the phrase accurately describes Teresa Heinz Kerry (from Mozambique) but not Colin Powell (of Jamaican descent). I literally didn't know the words to say, so I found myself taking the path of least resistance and not interacting honestly with others. This cannot be what the inventors of political correctness had in mind, creating such a tinderbox of language that racial differences are even more profound and exaggerated.

I took the kids to the public library for a puppet show commemorating Martin Luther King Day. The puppeteer wore an orange silk tunic and a hat the shape of a flowerpot, and my kids nestled into my lap as I sat cross-legged on the floor in the front row. We used to call this position "Indian-style," but Camille was instructed at school to call it the "crisscross applesauce" position. (Political correctness takes so-called offensive language, rids it of any contextual meaning, and multiplies the number of syllables to make sure the speaker is fervent enough to sound absurd. If you don't believe me, you've never witnessed a five-year-old's stammering attempt to describe her "African American" playmate who's actually from Haiti.) At any rate, the puppeteer told the uncensored story of the struggle for civil rights—about Rosa Parks's courageous refusal to move to the back of the bus, about the Birmingham fire hoses being used against protesters, and about a little speech called "I Have a Dream." However, he never said the word "Southerner" without preceding it with the descriptors "evil" and "white." Every time he said the phrase, Camille—who was very aware of her heritage—looked up at me in perplexity.

Later, when we planned a trip to Tennessee, she sat on her suitcase and refused to pack. "I'm scared, Mommy."

"Why?"

"It's dangerous in the South, right?"

Camille lived in the middle of the fifth largest city in America. In the past year, one woman had been randomly shot in the head on her way to work in front of our building, one guy was shot four times by police at a bus stop we'd just left, and another woman was raped in the subway in Chinatown near our apartment. Although Camille did see the bullet holes and police outline of the man, she hadn't quite understood why everyone was milling around the news vans and reporters. And since she's not allowed to watch the news, she didn't know about the female victims. But after attending Philadelphia public school for one year of kindergarten, she was certain of one thing—the South is a very scary place.

We sat crisscross applesauce on the bed—our knees touching and holding hands—and had a long talk. I wasn't offended at the puppeteer's using that phrase. The people to whom he was referring probably fit the bill in all three categories—evil, white, and Southern. But it was just too easy for kids to leave the library that day without realizing "evilwhitesoutherner" wasn't just one word—they didn't necessarily have to follow each other.

I resented having to defend myself to people around Philadelphia, who prejudged that I was prejudiced just because of my heritage. The fashionable anti-Semitism, the inability of my African American friend to get a cab to pick her up in New York, and the mass exodus of whites from Philadelphia's public schools make me realize the North doesn't have race figured out either. In fact, Philly is just as segregated as the South, if not more so.

In the car on the way home from Mocha Moms, Jacqueline and I sat in the if-the-glove-doesn't-fit-you-must-acquit silence for a while before making a pact. We agreed we'd be both candid and gracious to each other regarding racial issues. One year later, we still didn't agree on Colin Powell or Condoleezza, but I did know exactly how long it takes to get hair extensions. In fact, it was fun, and I regret advising Camille not to ever mention race. Ignoring skin color seems to put race in the same category as a facial zit, a blemish to overlook instead of part of God's multifaceted, diverse creation. I think I'll tell her next time to be brave and be kind and hope that people can develop thicker skin, no matter what its color.

God

I'm not normally a religious man, but if you're up there, save me, Superman!

—*Homer Simpson*

The Real Rainbow Coalition

IN NEW YORK, I attended an interdenominational church located at 51st Street and Broadway called Times Square Church, even though the blue awning over the entrance proclaimed "The Church That Love Is Building." I mean, honestly. Love? In a church? It seemed a little far-fetched to me, but over eight thousand people gathered to worship in the old Broadway theater every week, some of them driving more than two hours and staying for all three services. Being in New York was so spiritually disorienting that had there been tire swings instead of pews or jugglers instead of a preacher, I wouldn't have noticed.

Times Square Church is a "charismatic" church (from the Greek word for "gift"), meaning one that believes the miracles experienced by the apostles of the first-century church—healing, visions, prophecy, etc.—are available to modern Christians. Over a hundred nationalities worshipped at Times Square Church, however, and I couldn't tell the tongues of angels from Swahili or Gaelic. My high school Latin didn't help—since no one was translating Virgil or singing "Happy Birthday"—and so the disparate languages melded together into what I imagined to be the very sound of holiness. It contrasted jarringly with the neon decadence of nearby Times Square. In some churches, people arrive early to shake hands, talk about work, and drink coffee. But the congregants of this church came to pray, books embossed with the words "*Heilige Schrift*," "*Santa Biblia*," "*Bijbel*," or "Holy Bible" opened in their laps. In fact, a half hour before the opening song, only balcony seats would still be available. I never saw the main floor up close.

But what I could see of it startled me. The faithful were down there, crowding the stage, raising their hands in prayer. There was an elderly black man who stood on the floor to the left of the podium who simply yelled "Jesus! Jesus! Jesus!" over and over until the service began (and even intermittently throughout the sermon, like some people say amen). His staccato chant combined with the anguished prayers of women either terrified me or electrified me, but either way I was content to observe from the balcony.

The first time we were there, Pastor David Wilkerson said, "Ladies, when we stand to sing, please don't leave your pocketbooks on the ground. Some thieves are here in the sanctuary, so keep an eye out for your belongings. And for those of you who came here expressly to steal," he said, "we welcome you. You came here thinking you'd leave with a few bucks, but you'll leave knowing the life-changing love of God. Stay as long as you'd like."

I stayed in that seat after the sermon was over and watched as a hundred people responded to the messages by crowding the stage where Pastor David gently prayed, arms outstretched like he was receiving his grandchildren. Every week, his sermons

caused mobs of weeping people to come forward from the bal-
conies, from the main floor, and even from the overflow room
where people watched him on televisions. Times Square Church
emphasized giving aid to the poor, the hungry, and the addicted,
so the congregation was always full of strange-looking people.
One Sunday you might sit between an investment banker who
graduated from Princeton and an unemployed garbage collector.
I remember in the middle of one sermon Pastor David asked anyone who had attempted suicide or been addicted to drugs to
stand. I think everyone was shocked to see all over the sanctuary the hundreds of people of every economic level get out of
their seats—men in ties, men in short-sleeved polyester shirts,
and men with hair so greasy it stained their already soiled shirts.
This church did not overlook sin in order to maintain the appearance of godliness. It was after the real thing, challenging you
to look deep into your soul and extricate hidden vice. If Jesus
was the Great Physician, then this church was the hospital,
filled with hurting people staggering under the weight of their
problems.

I used to think that if anything deserved contempt in the
church, it was "emotionalism"—a catchall term to describe anything that deviated from the standard two hymns, a prayer, another hymn, and a twenty-two-minute sermon. Certainly you
could be thankful Jesus died for your sins, but showing it in any
way other than a furrowed brow during Communion demonstrated nothing but a weak mind. Even though Times Square
Church was miles away from my Tennessee church—in more
ways than geographically—I felt at home there, sitting in my red
velvet seat in the sometimes uncomfortable presence of God. I

closed my eyes during "Amazing Grace," heard people all around me singing in their native tongues, and knew exactly what heaven would sound like.

I went to church twice a week, even on Tuesday nights when David was working, and I dragged our friend Damon with me. We sat in the balcony, straining our eyes to see Pastor David in his blue suit. Many years later, I saw a head shot of him in a magazine and had no idea who he was. . . . I knew only his voice.

That voice. It exuded the goodness of God for almost seventy years, boiling down abstract theological concepts into practical help for thousands of New Yorkers. In its soft timbre, you could imagine it soothing mourners, reprimanding children, and advising hopeful newlyweds. Pastor David frequently forgot to turn off his lapel microphone, broadcasting his voice over the whole sanctuary while people rushed forward for prayer—eager to repent or keen on getting him to stop singing. His voice skipped notes, butchered lyrics, and fumbled over Bible passages. It wasn't silky like a newscaster's, and it frequently cracked under the strain of compassion. When angry, it split open your soul, like a disappointed grandfather who found you smoking behind the barn. It was strong and commanding, yet delivered the Gospel with the delicacy and tenderness of a child. And when it erupted into laughter, it was like rain on windowsills, as light and sweet as cotton candy.

Hearing that voice every week confounded, sobered, and changed me little by little, month by month. I especially enjoyed the worship. Two short, stout black women led the congregation, singing with such power that demons ran off horrified as soon as their mouths opened. There, if the Spirit prompted you to stand, you stood. If you felt like kneeling, you knelt. Some people cried, some people laughed, some people clapped. And the one guy in the corner kept screaming the name of Jesus. It was a bit odd, people everywhere *reacting* to God. I'd spent my whole life singing lyrics like "I will rejoice for He has made me glad!" as a funeral dirge and "I lift my hands to worship You" with my arms stubbornly crossed over my chest like a straitjacket. However, this church had a way of stripping away self-consciousness like little snakes of old paint. At Times Square, congregants were poor, many were hurt, and some even seemed a tad imbalanced. However, if Christianity was true, dancing in the aisles was an understandable and appropriate response. If it was false, then it'd be totally unimportant, just a historical footnote not worth considering. The one thing Christianity could not be was marginally important. And that's how I'd lived my entire life—with panty hose, high heels, and an emotional disconnect to preserve my dignity. I began to wonder who was crazy.

Times Square Church was not a typical Northeastern church. In fact, it's a downright anomaly, since New York has one of the lowest percentages of evangelicals in America. I've noticed that traffic conditions on Sunday mornings are a pretty good indication of an area's spiritual composition. In Nashville, for example, police are assigned outside the mega-congregations to make sure the thousands of people who are trying to get into church parking lots don't play demolition derby with their mini-vans and Tahoes. However, in Manhattan, an unintended gesture might cause three cabs to do U-turns to get your business on those desolate mornings. Recently, the Christian research organization the Barna Group found the four states with the lowest percentages of adult Christians were all resoundingly in the Northeast.

This is probably no surprise. If all America's fifteen million adult evangelicals were equally distributed geographically, there'd be no need for pejorative terms like "the Bible Belt," "Jesus Land," and—conversely—"Lost Angeles." What is surprising, at least to me, is how few Christians live in the Northeast. For example, Los Angeles (an area not known for its family values) has more evangelicals than New York, Chicago, and Boston *combined.*

As derisively as some people use the phrase "the Bible Belt," it's actually a pretty accurate description of the South: the ten areas in which at least six out of ten adults describe themselves as "born again" are all located in these red states. Southerners are more likely to commit to Christianity, read the Bible, attend Sunday school, and have a personal devotional time. They're also more likely to be born again (50 percent versus 39 percent in the rest of the nation) and evangelical (10 percent versus 5 percent in the rest of America).

Northeasterners are the least likely to do these things. Interestingly, 83 percent of adults in Jackson, Mississippi, are evangelicals, whereas the lowest percentages are in Boston and Providence.

The report had other interesting findings:

- Believing God is "the all-knowing, all-powerful creator of the universe who still rules it today" is most prevalent in Tulsa—located in Oklahoma (a red state)—and is least common in Boston and San Francisco (blue areas).

- Massachusetts, Connecticut, and Washington (blue areas) had almost double the national average of atheists and agnostics—one out of every six residents. However, atheists and agnostics are hardest to find in Louisiana (red) and Missouri (red).
- Alabama boasts the highest percentage of evangelical adults, with almost double the national average. Connecticut has the lowest, with just 26,000 of them in a state of more than two and a half million adults. Among states with higher populations, Massachusetts had the lowest percentage of "born again" adults by far (17%).[1]

In other words, the Northeast can be a pretty lonely place for evangelical Christians. As much as I love Philadelphia, I constantly hear the same refrain from people after they realize I'm an evangelical: "I've never actually met anyone who's a Christian." Of course, there are old churches in the city, but they frequently don't believe in the Bible the same way most Southern churches do—namely that it's true. The perfect example of this was a Gothic Episcopal church near our Philadelphia home built on the site that Benjamin Franklin flew his famous kite. On its outside walls, above the historical commemorative plaque, was a quote from a Buddhist religious document, another from an agnostic American playwright, and a gay pride symbol. I noticed they were holding a Tibetan Chenrezig prayer ceremony—to encourage "world peace and compassion"—which was to be conducted by Buddhist monks. And this church was not atypical of the churches in Philadelphia.

One of the oldest churches in the nation is Christ Church of

Philadelphia, which was established in 1695. In fact, it's sometimes called "America's Church" because of its intimate association with the people who created this country—George and Martha Washington, Benjamin Franklin, and Betsy Ross all worshipped there. Recently, I was at a friend's place and I happened to pick up the church's bulletin. In it were the normal things that fill church bulletins—meeting times, birth announcements, prayer requests. I read that Gene Robinson—the first openly noncelibate gay priest to be ordained a bishop in the Anglican community—was coming to Philadelphia to celebrate gay rights and was holding a special service for gays, lesbians, and the transgendered. This differentiated it slightly from the typical Southern church bulletin announcing afternoon potluck and admonishing kids not to hog the chicken salad. But when I began to read the message from the rector, I was shocked to see that he compared Christians who don't accept homosexuality to Nazis. (Since then, I've learned he also believes Jesus was not sinless but used "hate speech" and racial slurs.) With Christians like this, who needs atheists?

It's a little overwhelming. I was once wandering around Manhattan alone while David worked late in his office. I was quickly becoming distressed at the chaos, the drugs in Washington Square Park, and the depravity that loomed all around me in Times Square. Then, suddenly, I heard a lone voice above the rest of the clamor. "Jesus! Jesus! Jesus!" Its tone and pitch were so abrasive I knew it immediately. I got a little closer and saw him standing on the corner, dressed in a suit, tie, and a wide-brimmed hat, smiling from ear to ear at passersby and swaying like Ray Charles as he yelled the name of his savior. Since I always sat in the balcony, I'd never seen his face before . . . always wanting a little distance between me and people who seemed to love God with the same fervor with which addicts love cocaine. Suddenly I realized that even though we were different colors, ages, and genders, I had more in common with him than with most people in New York. The real difference between me and that gentleman was that I held my arms out to protect myself, whereas he held his arms wide open to embrace a city that didn't embrace him back. I couldn't stop staring at him, at his joy and apparent disregard for the contempt people exuded as they walked by. And his ability to reduce two thousand years' worth of theology into one striking word just broke me wide open.

The Ultimate Overdrive Xperience

"DO YOU WANT to go to the traditional service or"—David looked up at me from the church Web site on his computer—"'the Ultimate Overdrive Xperience'?"

It was our first week living in a small town in Tennessee, and we realized late Saturday night that we had no idea where to go to church the next morning. The boxes were unpacked and the curtains were hung, so we decided to go ahead and begin the torturous process of shopping around for a church. Without knowing anyone in the area for referrals, we settled on a Baptist church we found online.

"The what?"

He cleared his throat. "The Ultimate Overdrive Xperience, with a capital X. It's for . . . 'people who can't stand religion' and are 'sick of hypocritical people.'"

"Now that you mention it, I *am* a little sick of hypocritical people. Go on."

He read directly from the Web site. "'So, you think church is boring or irrelevant? Then Xperience is for you. The only thing to expect is the unexpected.'"

In the South, the culture is so saturated with Christianity that churches strive to differentiate themselves from other churches by promising something out of the ordinary. In fact, many churches intentionally dress down, serve coffee in the back, and try at all costs to avoid "churchiness." Since David and I aren't surprised to see coaches at high school football games, violins in an orchestra, and a little "churchiness" in church, we normally just go ahead and attend regular services. However, one thing always trumps our desire for church tradition: sleeping in. And since the normal service was at the crack of dawn—nine o'clock—we were destined for the 10:30 Overdrive Xperience.

"Baptist Church: Empowering People to Meet Relevant Needs," read the sign above the parking lot.

"I guess that's better than empowering people to gratify extraneous desires," David said as we pulled into an entire section of parking spaces reserved for first- and second-time visitors. The children bounded into their brightly painted, balloon-bedecked classrooms, after we filled in information sheets at the front desk.

"Don't put our real phone numbers down," I whispered to David, who rolled his eyes and accused me of cynicism.

The praise band was playing loud songs the lead singer had written, which meant the five hundred or so congregants stood lamely at their seats, looking slightly bewildered at the unfamiliar lyrics. His image was projected on a giant Jumbotron screen for the benefit of the people in the back of the auditorium, but I couldn't stop looking at his apparel—jeans, a T-shirt, and inexplicably, a terry cloth wristband with a Superman emblem.

"He's not wearing shoes," I pointed out to David, although it must have been dress-up Sunday since he was wearing socks.

"Will you at least try to concentrate on what's important?"

The answer was no, I definitely could not. The seats were comfortably padded, the sanctuary nice and roomy, but the words of the song—the ones I could understand—were not bringing me into the presence of the Almighty. Like many churches, this one had traded the old hymns that included outdated phrases like "here I raise my Ebenezer" with newer choruses with phrases like "His return is very close, so you better be believing."

I have room in my heart for both the old and new, or so I thought. As our spiritual Superman led us in his songs, he crooned, "These words are from the heart, Lord. They are not made up."

I gave a sideways glance at David to see if he was trying to figure out how lyrics being projected across the bottom of the screen from a computer in the back of the room and being sung by five hundred people could be made up on the spur of the moment, but he was singing happily—obviously not a victim of a sarcastic heart.

At long merciful last, the pastor got up at the podium and welcomed us to the service. "We're just so glad you're here," he said. "And now we're going to do something that's a big Bible word: *fellowshipping.*" At this I involuntarily snorted and David scooted away from me in the pew. Some churches, in a well-intentioned effort not to be off-putting to newcomers who might not know the traditional church jargon—like "transubstantiation," "incarnate," and "potluck"—avoid using Christian vocabulary altogether. This is good in theory, but when he said "big Bible word," it cracked me up in the powerfully forbidden way that occurs only during church. Most churches also have abandoned the "thees" and "thous" of the King James Version of the Bible for more modern translations. Instead of the commonly known "For God so loved the world that he gave his only begotten Son," for example, newer versions begin John 3:16 with the more contemporary "God was showin' you some love and makin' you his dawg by givin' up his shorty. . . ."

In continuation of his fellowship theme, the pastor made everyone stand to meet new visitors, which is a little less comfortable than dental surgery with blunt instruments. This forced fellowship is designed to make visitors feel welcome, but sometimes makes them feel like the last kid waiting to be picked for the kickball team. We stood up, as people passed us in the aisles, greeting friends and family members all around us. The people with the misfortune of sitting in front of us turned around, shook our hands with limp grips, and turned back around a few syllables into our greeting: "Hi, we're the Frenches, and we're new—"

Then, nothing but the backs of their heads. You can't blame them for not wanting to strike up a conversation with strangers during a two-and-a-half-minute interval. The stand-up-and-talk-to-someone-you-don't-know routine was probably the innovative idea of some pastor in Toledo, but now—no doubt after books and video series touted the practice—most churches do it.

In fact, fads take hold so quickly in the evangelical world that you can go to almost any evangelical church and find people with The Purpose-Driven Life tucked under arms or in purses. And when we had children and found ourselves in disagreement with the trendy Christian parenting book, we were reduced to the embarrassing admission that we weren't, in fact, *Growing Kids God's Way*. In the early nineties, the fashion was to replace old hymnals with overhead projection screens to spare the congregation the effort of picking up the book and having to turn the pages—in ten years, the plan is to roll people in and out of the church on sleeper sofas and give them straws with Communion so they won't have to ever sit upright.

The tricky part about the overhead projection screens is that their utility depends on the skill and attention of the people working them. The lady who was responsible for switching the transparencies between verses at my church in Kentucky evidently got so wrapped up in her own worship that she frequently was one or two verses behind, resulting in more slurred words in church than in a bar on Saturday night. Worse, the transparencies also had distracting spelling errors that caused my mind to wander from God to reality television to the gym: "Amazing race, how sweat the sound . . ."

Since hands were free of those cumbersome hymnals, worship leaders sometimes encouraged participation by asking you to, for example, "hug the neck of your neighbor and tell them you're happy to see them." I, of course, always refused to do this as a matter of principle—making me look like the most unspiritual person in the room and making the person next to me look the most unappreciated.

But if you've ever regularly attended church services in the South, you've probably had more than your share of uncomfortable moments. You've held the perspiring hands of people you don't know across the aisles during the very long prayers of well-

meaning pastors. You've read *The Prayer of Jabez* or heard at least
three sermons on it. You've shouted "Jesus" at the top of your
lungs for a worship leader who doesn't think the congregation is
fervent enough. You've sung the verses of "Just as I Am" three
million seven hundred and eighty-one times. You've enthusias-
tically applauded children's Christmas plays just because they finally ended. You've sung the phrase "for such a worm as I."
You've wondered what would happen if you took money *out* of
the collection plate. You've attended special singing services
that make you long for the candor of Simon Cowell. You've sung
"Joy to the World" in July to make the point that people should
celebrate the birth of Christ all year round. You've fallen asleep
mid-sermon and tried to pass it off as being emotionally moved.
You've realized it's physically impossible to make your stomach
stop growling once it gets going. You've gotten pulled over for
speeding on the way to church as other members drive by and
wave. You've pretended it wasn't your cell phone playing "Für
Elise" during Communion. You have no idea how a fish came to
symbolize Christianity but still had to repent over fantasies of
rear-ending the jerk driving in front of you with the Darwin
decal. You've participated in Holy Spirit conga lines around the
church, danced to songs proclaiming "the river is here," and
fought the urge to throw a study Bible at the song leader the
twentieth time he tells the choir to "do that verse once more."
And, if you're like me, you've unsuccessfully suppressed giggles
after someone testified that his hemorrhoids have been healed
by a "touch from the Lord."

Just as Northerners speak in code, Southerners also have a
way of speaking that can seem perfectly innocuous if you aren't

attuned to the hidden meaning. The sweetly uttered "Noticed you weren't at church on Sunday. Everything okay, hon?" from a hairnetted lady in the grocery store is really code for "Have you fallen away from the Lord, or are you just spiritually lazy?" In other words, church attendance is considered a little more crucial than court appearances, and the general feeling is that if you neglect church, you'll probably end up living a life of crime anyway. And not just a pleasantly short Sunday morning admonition from the preacher not to cheat on your taxes. The church in the South has apparently not gotten the memo that there are other things in life that people might want to do, like spend time with family, or—God forbid—watch the Super Bowl. Most churches have what some might call cruel sleep deprivation, but is referred to in the propagandist bulletin as Sunday school. This is followed by a sermon and worship, usually accompanied by the angelic sound of hundreds of stomachs growling in harmony. Of course, there's a Wednesday evening service that is a little less casual and like all Sunday's services squished into one. Not to mention the revivals that take place intermittently on the weekends that require not only your presence but your enthusiasm.

The question "Do you go to church?" is almost never asked in the South, but rather "Where do you go to church?" Then, depending on your answer, there's usually a follow-up question. If you say, "Presbyterian," then you're asked, "PCA or PCUSA?" If you respond "Baptist," then the question is "Southern?" It's a little like how animals are classified from broad terms to the more specific. In the spiritual taxonomy, for example, I might be classified as a part of the *kingdom* of Christianity, the *phylum* of

Protestant, the *class* of Evangelical, the *order* of Calvin, the *family* of Presbyterian, the *genus* of Presbyterian of America, and the *species* of Very Confused About Infant Baptism.

In the North, these distinctions are virtually meaningless—orthodox Christians are so rare, you have an instant bond with any believer. In the South, however, you have the luxury of picking and choosing a church that meets your exact spiritual needs. Churches of the same denomination will sit across the street from each other, divided long ago over the issue of whether to have Sunday school programs for kids, whether to use grape juice or wine in Communion, or what color to paint the vestibule. So no matter what beliefs you develop over the course of your lifetime, you can usually find hundreds of others who share those precise convictions.

And everyone's beliefs are certainly works in progress. I was baptized at the age of twelve in a swimming pool at Mid-South Youth Camp in Henderson, Tennessee, by head counselor John McCaskill. Since baptism was of primal importance to my denomination (I grew up in the Church of Christ, a sect that believes one should never worship the Lord with musical accompaniment), any water deep enough for immersion was utilized to facilitate immediate obedience. I was thankful they didn't dunk me in the dank pond normally used for canoeing and the occasional prank involving campers' underwear. My parents and friends stood at the side of the pool as John asked me if I believed Jesus was the son of God before placing a white cloth over my face and gently lowering me into the cold water. I remember the crisp bite of the water engulfing me, and I made sure all my body got wet, so a wayward limb wouldn't stick out and invalidate the whole thing. I fell asleep with damp hair on the top bunk of cabin 3, smelling faintly of chlorine and feeling lighter than helium.

Within weeks, however, I'd gone back to the old life of my twelve-year-old sin. For some reason—I think to make my friends laugh—I said "damn" at a football game. I was so inexperienced at profanity that I lacked the confidence to even lose my temper. My motto was "Profanity is for those who lack the intelligence to otherwise express themselves" (which made me sound smart *and* moral) until that night when "damn" slipped out of my mouth as easily as if I were a shock jock on XM Radio.

The next time the "song of invitation" was being sung at church, I knew exactly what I had to do. The "song of invitation" was the last hymn sung during our worship service, following the sermon, when anyone in the congregation who wanted to publicly repent of a sin could make the long walk down the aisle to do so. The Catholic church had confessional booths, but my church had the long walk of shame. This was not a frequent occurrence (not many people were brave enough to run the gauntlet, no matter how grievous their sin), so when "Just as I Am" began, everyone sang on autopilot, thinking about lunch plans and negotiating which parent would pick up the kids from the nursery. Until, of course, they saw me starting down the aisle. At which point, necks craned and imaginations ran wild with speculation about what was sinful enough to cause me to humiliate myself so publicly.

It took me until the second verse to build up enough nerve to do it. "Just as I am and waiting not . . ." As soon as I placed my right foot on the green carpet, I knew I'd made a grave mistake. "To rid my soul of one dark blot . . ." If there'd been a video of the moment, it would've appeared I had some sort of mobility problem and that I was going forward to be healed of a disease that prohibited my legs from cooperating with each other. In fact, I could garner only enough willpower to move one foot at a time past all the people glancing sideways from their hymnals to the adolescent girl with feet of lead. "To Thee whose blood can cleanse each spot . . ." Since most people don't "go forward" for sins unless they were already public knowledge—like pregnancy or public drunkenness—the congregation held its breath until I finally made it to the preacher. "O Lamb of God, I come, I come." To his credit, the preacher—a rotund and jovial B. B. James, who looked even more surprised at my response than I was—received me with open arms and ushered me to the front pew. As the song leader scrambled to find another hymn, stomachs growled for lunch, and people turned to look at the clock hanging in the back of the auditorium, I quickly glanced over the options.

Would you like
A. to get baptized, B. to rededicate yourself to the Lord,
or C. to make a confession of sin?

I circled the C but couldn't force myself to elaborate, having exhausted my reserve of willpower to get myself down the aisle. I hesitated before handing it back, wondering momentarily if I should scribble, "Said 'damn' at football game," but I felt the eyes of the people behind me trying to look over my shoulder, so I shoved the card at Brother James. He talked briefly about how

God is happy to forgive us of any sin we might commit in a generic speech that would've been appropriate for both profanity and tax evasion, and that was that. After church, I told my curious family of my terrible transgression, and my mother rolled her eyes while my sisters giggled. Later at lunch, I knocked my drink over on the table, and my sister Amy said, "Maybe you should just go forward at church next week."

In other words, I had some of the basics of Christianity a little wrong. Not only did I think you had to publicly confess every single sin, I also believed—after growing up in Kentucky—that "tobacco" was a book in the Old Testament (confusing it with Habakkuk).

Everyone in the South has theological issues they're working out. Growing up in a culture of Christianity, actually, is like having a gigantic dysfunctional family—instead of "hugging the neck" of the Christian standing beside you, you might sometimes prefer to wring it. Like real families, we have freeloading members who try to talk people out of money and crazy uncles who refuse to quit talking long after they stop making sense. Christianity, however, is not a simple matter of following directions or interpreting a document—it's really nothing more than a conglomeration of many imperfect relationships between individuals and their Creator, making its survival thus far nothing short of miraculous.

I grew up attending the improbably named Sulphur Well Church of Christ, near Paris Landing at Kentucky Lake. It was named after an artesian well of sulphur water accidentally struck in 1821 during an attempt to find a salt bed on a Chickasaw reservation. People flocked to the site—believing the smelly water had medicinal value—and sought refuge there during the 1837 yellow fever epidemic. In 1944, the well was covered by the creation of Kentucky Lake, one of the country's largest man-made lakes, and my church was formed right near that old well.

In the Bible, sulphur is called brimstone—because it's frequently found on the brims of volcanoes—and a rain of it destroyed Sodom and Gomorrah. But in spite of being named after a tool of eternal destruction, Sulphur Well was a good church— no longer smelling of sulphur but just of the reeking pig farm downwind. A few families comprised more than half the congregation and had worshipped together happily for many generations. But this didn't stop the Wimberleys, Clendenins, Stephens, Milams, and Crocketts (descendants of Davy, although they lost their coonskin caps years ago) from welcoming us newcomers with open arms. The tiny country church with a half-empty auditorium (or was it half full?) eventually had folding chairs lining the aisles and a Sunday school room shortage. But when the preacher adopted the motto "Welcome to Sulphur Well, where there's always room for one more," he kept his promise. They did what needed to be done to accommodate the new crowds and never made us feel like intruders. George Milam taught our high school group and timidly broached subjects like sex and drinking with a look of utter terror in his eyes. And we definitely didn't let him off easy. One time, in Sunday school, an elder was teaching us against evolution when a slip of the tongue caused him to say "orgasms" instead of "organisms." Only two of us were alert enough to notice, and Jason Wimberley convulsed so violently holding in his laughter he was accused of being Pentecostal. The fact that we still talk about it to this day, fifteen years later, is probably a testimony to how ordinary life there was. It was the type of place where no one raised an eyebrow about Oscar Clendenin riding his horse to church or my dad greeting everyone with a friendly "howdydosir" regardless of their gender.

The preacher, Randy Stephens, uses sayings from the pulpit like "let's tie a string around it" to summarize his point, and if the teenagers aren't paying attention in the back row, he says, "I'm gonna repeat myself because I think three of you missed that." He closes his sermons by saying, "I hope this message scratched where ya itched," and—instead of asking us to meditate on the theme—he might encourage us to "chew on it for a while."

People brought casseroles to shut-ins, sang at the nursing home, and called if you were sick. The youth group secretly played spin the bottle, had devotionals, ate pizza off plastic plates in the fellowship hall, and commiserated our way through the shock of puberty. Years later, after I'd moved far away, the congregation threw a wedding shower for David and me—even though I know a few had reservations over my marrying so quickly. Mr. Oscar gave me a pizza cutter which is still in my drawer ten years later, a small reminder of the church's attentiveness to even our most basic needs. All in all, this "typical church" was not a bad place to grow up.

Perhaps my affection for that straightforward country church makes me view the amped-up services like the Overdrive Xperience with too much skepticism. Simply put, the Southern church's, ahem, Xcessive willingness to reach out to the community and adapt to meet cultural needs—while still maintaining a firm grasp on the truth of Scripture—is one of the ways it maintains relevancy in today's society. Even as other regions collectively reject the faith of their fathers, the Southern church remains a vibrant—if perhaps quirky—place to be. It's also pretty reliably a place where people "hug your neck" and are always "glad to see you," which, at the risk of using big biblical terminology, just might scratch where you itch.

Cheese and Rice

IN THE SOUTH, profanity was called "cussing," and my high school friends did it with a skill and creativity never applied to other aspects of their lives. After repenting of my football game infraction, however, I wasn't keen on picking up the habit again. Not only did I steer clear of any activity that might make me foolishly decide to go forward again at church, but also my high school identity had become interwoven with my anticussing beliefs. Brooke was the insecure yet beautiful Texas-born cheerleader, Olivia was the sweetheart with perfectly applied Mary Kay makeup, Nathan was the clever wise guy who never fit in with the jocks, and I was the student body president who didn't cuss. Letting the F word fly from my mouth would've been so out of character people would've just laughed, as if Al Gore entered a break dancing contest.

At home, my dad turned the television off if anything more strident than "shucks" was uttered by the characters. It didn't matter if Murdock was in the middle of rescuing the A-Team from Mexican drug lords, or if Mr. Roarke and Tattoo were about to make someone's fantasy vacation come true. Whenever an objectionable word was uttered, my dad took a long, disappointed walk across the living room and turned the little knob until it clicked—at which point, we'd break out the Uno cards. This made it very difficult to participate in conversations about popular culture, as I always had inadequate information. I didn't know if Sam was able to convince Diane to marry him in *Cheers* or if KITT rescued Michael Knight by using his smoke bombs, infrared sensors, or flamethrowers. When people talked about the shows, I'd be reduced to the noncommittal yet enthusiastic "It was amazing!" However, if a close examination of their faces indicated the ending wasn't actually amazing but rather disappointing, I'd add soberly, "and rather sad, really, how things work out."

I even got yanked off the tire swing and spanked when my mom overheard me repeating the message of a birthday card on my teacher's desk: "Lordy, Lordy, Mrs. Pittman's Forty!" Evidently, we weren't supposed to say "damn" *or* use God's name in vain. As a member of a very conservative church, however, I was unaware that God's name was, in fact, Lordy. My denomination was so reserved, I'd heard God addressed only as the temperate "Dear Heavenly Father." Invariably, I equated "Lord" with "Have you gained a few pounds?"—on the never-to-be-uttered list. In music class, I was terrified to sing, "When the Saints Go Marching In," because I thought the line "Oh Lord, I want to be in that number" was as offensive as Alanis Morissette singing about her movie theater exploits. I began to resent my music teacher leading us down the path of destruction, so I slurred the words and prayed God wasn't paying attention.

After I got out of high school, the level of profanity I heard dropped off considerably. In fact, polite company demanded a strict code of ethics relating to cussing—mainly that you use it only when absolutely necessary and never in mixed company. Manners on this were strictly enforced, so a violator would likely be slapped in the head and asked rhetorically, "Don't you see there's a lady present?"

Many years later, David and I volunteered with the youth group at Trinity Assembly of God in Georgetown, Kentucky, and were assigned small groups. My girls weren't the "church" type, didn't wear Izod shirts, and didn't participate in extracurricular activities to pad their college applications. Instead, they had no aspirations, ghastly black hair, and jewelry favoring the skull motif. We talked about God at Mexican dives where they'd stiff the waiter because he couldn't speak English. I taught them about Jesus and restaurant etiquette, and even had black T-shirts made with the ironic name we'd chosen for ourselves: the Righteous Sisters. Within weeks, my group was attracting foster kids, Satan worshippers, and other malcontents who gave fake names, threw their hands in the air in mock worship, and e-mailed me afterward seeking advice about boyfriends, salvation, and how to quit smoking. In spite of my best efforts, they were drawn to me and I became the pied piper of the bathing impaired. Gradually, our youth services began to look like a club scene.

When the youth pastor asked David to lead Sunday school, he decided to start with basics. "Is Christianity Boring, Untrue, or Irrelevant?" was the first class he taught, followed by "Who Is Jesus?" and "Why Did He Die?" After two months, we were ready to tackle the topic of the Holy Spirit, which generated so much interest among the kids we decided to do a weekend retreat on it at Center Hill Lake. The girls and I had an agreement—we could talk about any subject, as long as they didn't tie me up while I slept and tattoo me. I could tell this wasn't going to be your mother's Holy Spirit weekend when I met the girls' boyfriends—a disgusting lot of guys who apparently eschewed the sun like they did oral hygiene. One guy in particular, named Shane, thought he was a charmer, but I liked him less than a good cavity. He carried himself with a totally unfounded confidence because his family had received a million-dollar legal settlement that was spent within two years on a nicer double-wide, a Dodge Ram extended cab, and hundreds of lottery tickets (after all, it takes money to make money). The thing that really bothered me was the overt sexual attention he lavished on my fifteen-year-old Righteous Sisters, several of whom had more sexual experience than Jenna Jameson.

Somehow I was able to resist his charms and refused to buy him cigarettes on the way to the lake. When we got there, he brought out a large collection of Marilyn Manson CDs and proceeded to play them on the cabin's CD player, allowing the most offensive, profane words to waft over the young girls in my charge.

"Turn it off," I demanded. He laughed like I was the biggest prude and started mouthing off about how I was needlessly censoring him. "It's just words," he said. "They don't mean anything."

"Really?" I asked.

"Yeah. We're from a different generation. Kids my age don't even notice 'em."

"Well, f——k you."

Immediately I wished I could catch the words on their voyage between my lips and everyone's ears. But as soon as I turned the CD player off, I realized the room was as silent as a morgue. The ice maker in the refrigerator turned on in the adjacent kitchen, the pendulum on the mantel clock ticked softly, and the wings of the hummingbirds on the porch buzzed like bumblebees. The loudest sound, however, was a thud that came from behind the door of a bedroom—the sound of our youth pastor's jaw hitting the floor.

"See?" I tossed the CD into Shane's lap. "Words do affect people. So don't let me hear that kind of language again."

That kind of shock value isn't achievable in places like Philadelphia, where profanity is used with the regularity of Metamucil. Mothers used the S word, the D word, and even the F word in front of tiny, listening ears. I had to have several conversations with the kids about how we don't use words like those, and one afternoon, the inevitable happened. Camille came tearing down the steps at Rene's house, saying, "Ethan said the G word!"

I could tell the other mothers, who were going through their mental list of expletives, were coming up with no g's. I whispered that other parents have different rules for their kids, patted her bottom, and told her to take care of her own business.

"The G word is 'gosh,'" I said to Rene and Charlene, an agnostic Catholic, who looked at me as if I'd just announced I didn't let my children breathe air. I tried to explain that I hope my children avoid obscenity (inappropriate references to sexual activity), vulgarity (inappropriate references to bodily functions), and blasphemy (inappropriate references to aspects of God). Geoffrey Nunberg* put it most succinctly when he said

---

*Author of *Going Nucular: Language, Politics, and Culture in Controversial Times* and researcher at Stanford University's Center for the Study of Language and Information.

obscenity takes bedroom and bathroom activities and drags them out into the living room. Blasphemy, on the other hand, hauls heaven down into the common world.

Historical prohibitions against using religious words have caused a wealth of euphemisms, if they can be described in such a way. Almost all cartoons use words like "gosh," "gad," "golly," which are muted words for "God"; whereas "heck" and "Sam Hill" are substitutes for "hell." Batman and Robin say "holy cow!" and David Letterman even says "holy crap!" "Jiminy Christmas," "Jeez Louise," and even the Crocodile Hunter's "Crikey!" all attempt to avoid using the name of Jesus Christ. Some Christians go around saying the ridiculous "cheese and rice!" while others won't even say "hell." Flo, the beehived waitress on *Alice*, used to say to Mel, "Kiss my grits and go straight to H-E-double hockey sticks."

While I appreciate resisting blatant profanity, ridiculous euphemisms teach a holiness-by-technicality gospel I feel just isn't accurate. I don't teach the kids to have clean language to stave off a God full of retribution; rather, that disrespect and antagonism toward God will hurt their relationship with their loving Father. That's why I teach them to avoid words like "gosh," I explained to Rene, whose eyes by this time had glazed over with boredom.

"So, when my kindergartener yells out 'Jesus Christ, Mom! I'm famished,' you think that's bad?"

Recently a Jewish newspaper listed Madonna as one of the most influential Jews in America, which of course caused much controversy in the Jewish community. The editor defended himself by saying, "She's a practitioner of the kabbalah, so she's practicing Judaism, for Christ's sake!" before adding, "Well, not *really* for Christ's sake."[1] Likewise, Rene is more likely to believe the Department of Homeland Security is out to steal her credit card number than that Jesus was divine. So why—except perhaps in deference to Christians and Muslims—should her language patterns reflect a respect for Christ that's not in her heart?

"I don't care what your kids say," I said, "but my kids pray in the name of Jesus."

"Yeah," she said with a laugh, "and mine curse in his name."

"It's sad . . ." I began, thinking this issue perfectly exemplified the only but rather large chasm separating Rene and me. Last year, our kids decided to "fall out of love," when Camille realized Ethan wouldn't have a Christmas tree. And some of Rene's friends fell out of love with me when they discovered my politically conservative religious beliefs. It's the reason we spend hours talking on the phone, why we're constantly surprised at each other, and why I cherish her friendship. I noticed Rene smile at me from across the table, the steam from her coffee rising out of the mug when she drank. "And rather amazing, really, how things work out."

One Way to Heaven

RENE INVITED US to one of the oldest synagogues in America, B'nai Abraham in Philadelphia, for their Purim festivities. I don't know what I expected, actually. Perhaps I didn't notice the emphasis on "festivities." Purim, I learned, is the Jewish holiday observed each year on the fourteenth of Adar, celebrating the deliverance of the Jewish people from the wicked Haman by Queen Esther of Persia.

I was told the kids dress up in costumes, much like on Halloween. But as we walked up to the synagogue, I wondered if Rene was playing some sort of cruel Jewish joke on us. I had reluctantly dressed the kids as Sleeping Beauty and Buzz Lightyear but had a nagging suspicion we'd be the only ones in costumes— something that occurs with such frequency in movies and sitcoms I feared it just might happen in real life. I'd certainly never been to a synagogue before, but Sleeping Beauty offended even my sense of spiritual decorum.

I was wrong. The main ritual of Purim is the recitation in synagogue of the Scroll of Esther, which tells the story of Haman's attack on the Jews. In Hebrew. So my husband put on

a head covering, as is required, and we made our way to the sanctuary. Not being familiar with Jewish customs, I was afraid I was
inadvertently offending people by my presence or by accidentally brushing against someone in the crowded hallways. When
we made it into the sanctuary, we sat between a clown and a
woman in Moroccan garb who both appeared to be, as they say
in Hebrew, three sheets to the wind.

Several men at the front of the synagogue were chanting in
a kind of singsong from the Book of Esther which is known as
the megillah, or scroll. Suddenly the whole congregation started
yelling and spinning noisemakers called gragers each time the
reader mentioned Haman, the villain of the story. Everyone simultaneously booed, hissed, stamped their feet, and used cym-
bals, no small accomplishment since the story was entirely in
Hebrew. I never knew when to yell, but I followed the lead of
the people around me (which is also how I know when to ap-
plaud at a symphony).

Interestingly, on Purim you're supposed to drink enough
wine until you do not know the difference between *arur Haman*
and *baruch Mordechai* ("cursed Haman" and "blessed Mordechai").
(I reminded David that Christians don't celebrate this way even
if we are in a synagogue, according to the spiritual principle of
"sitting in a henhouse don't make you a hen.") There were
shouts of joy and dancing, and it struck me these Jews would feel
completely at home in a Pentecostal church, sans Jesus references and mullet hairdos.

The kids had their own festivities in the basement, where
they got to hear the megillah in English, giving them an unfair
advantage in knowing when to stomp and yell. They also made

little wooden hamsas, amulets that offer spiritual protection from the evil eye. I tried to figure out how many Christian principles this violated when the kids ran up with them in their glue-covered hands and yelled, "Look, Mom, we made Christmas ornaments!"

We had a lot to learn.

One day Rene brought her sons over for a playdate. Before they arrived, I rushed around cleaning up the Hot Wheels, Spider-Man figures, and innumerable drawings of mermaids that seem to multiply like Gremlins in a swimming pool. As I was making up the kids' bunk beds, I noticed an enormous poster hanging on the wall over their computer. I'd seen it a million times before, but I looked at it that day as if for the first time: it was shaped like a traffic sign and read "Jesus is the ONE WAY to Heaven," with an arrow pointing upward.

Camille had made it in vacation Bible school before we left Kentucky, and I'd stuck it on the wall without realizing a little Jewish boy who was just learning to read would one day be playing innocently beneath it. For a moment, I struggled over whether yanking it off the wall would indicate any shame of the gospel message on my part—I certainly believed in the claims of Christianity and also relished the privilege of sharing the gospel with people. However, as I stood there with my arms full of Batman costumes and Barbie outfits, I considered the logical implications of the sign. I certainly wouldn't have wanted Camille playing with Play-Doh under a sign that read "Jesus was a Blasphemer." Although Rene and I had explored for hours the spiritual heritage that both Jews and Christians share, it always

came down to the necessarily divisive belief about Christ. I
didn't want a playdate to turn into some sort of spiritual crisis for
a five-year-old, so I tore the poster off the wall and stuffed it
under their bunk beds. I wasn't denying Jesus, I told myself, I was
practicing the Golden Rule.

Rene and I were drinking coffee downstairs when I heard a
happy squeal from the loft area above us. "Mom! Look what fell
off the wall!" The pitter-pattering of little feet made my stomach
lurch, and I saw the top of the poster bouncing unevenly down
the staircase. "I want to show Mrs. Rene!"

There are moments in parenting that can define the lives of
children. My friend was baptized when he was eight years old
and afterward overheard his mother mumble, "He doesn't know
what he's doing." He consequently spent years doubting his con-
version.

In the fraction of a second I had to decide what to do, I
should've known better than to react harshly to Camille's small
demonstration of her love for Jesus, should've appreciated her
willingness to share her faith with friends, and should've encouraged her lack of self-consciousness. Instead, I jumped out of my
chair, threw myself between the poster and Rene, and practically
demolished the sign when I tried to shove it behind the entertainment center.

Even though Camille was stunned by my near acrobatic
moves, she perceived that she had done something wrong and
proceeded to burst into tears. "What on earth are you doing?"
both Rene and Camille wanted to know. Rene snatched the
poster from its hiding place and mouthed "Jesus is the one way
to Heaven." She smiled.

"You think I'm going to hell, don't you?" she asked after Camille was back upstairs.

"You can't trick me," I said. "You don't believe in hell."

"If I see Jesus coming out of the sky, I'll believe in Jesus," she assured me, "just in case there is a hell. You know what dry heat does to my skin."

Our conversations are about as dull as a drawer of Ginsu knives, cutting away predispositions in the most humorous and sometimes painful ways possible. Since meeting Rene, we've gone to Chanukah parties, to Jewish birthday parties, and to the Purim festivities. Now if my son wants his sister to scream, all he has to do is come up behind her and whisper "Haman," making us very popular with the neighbors in our building. For a time, the kids actually thought we were Jews. I tried to explain Christianity was once known as a Jewish sect but that it's now not considered Jewish. However, the similarities are too much for them to comprehend. We worship the same God, memorize the same Scriptures, and revere Jesus, who is a moderately famous Jew himself. And Queen Esther has always been Camille's hero. I've given up trying to convince them otherwise. Especially since they beg to return to the synagogue every week.

Next year, I told them. Purim is the perfect time to experience Judaism, as the story of Esther is an amazing tale of intrigue, courage, and the deliverance of God. And it resonates, no matter what your beliefs.

Stereotypes

We don't have milk cows. People have so many stereotypes of people from where I come from— Oklahoma. We don't ride around in covered wagons, either.

—*Carrie Underwood*

All stereotypes turn out to be true. This is a horrifying thing about life. All those things you fought against as a youth: you begin to realize they're stereotypes because they're true.

—*David Cronenberg*

The Best Way to Kill Squirrels

DOMINIC, A MAN who owned the shiny food cart outside my building in Philadelphia, serenades each of his regular customers with specially chosen songs based on occupation, hometown, or interests. For my son, he breaks into "Spider-Man, Spider-Man, does whatever a spider can . . ." For the guy from South Philly who always orders a cheesesteak, he'll sing, "The Eye of the Tiger" in honor of Rocky Balboa. He was at a loss when he met me, not knowing any Southern songs. I taught him the "Tennessee Waltz" after "Rocky Top" just refused to roll off his Yankee tongue—as disastrous as Rene's effort to teach me Yiddish. Now every time I walk by, I hear a heartfelt "I was waltzing with my darlin' to the Tennessee waltz, when an old friend, I happened to see . . ." Once, after he sang to me, a couple of guys in line asked, "You're from Tennessee? Does your husband hunt?"

Dominic interrupted. "What're you saying? She's a *true* Southern woman—I bet *she* hunts!"

This saved me from disappointing them with the revelation that David only plays paintball. I could tell they were impressed when I told them how my dad took us deer hunting when I was a kid to celebrate our birthdays. As our breaths crystallized in the cold morning air, I wondered if I could gut a deer like we'd been taught in science while Daddy silently raised his hands in the air, his fingers in the V shape for victory, and shook his head back and forth like Richard Nixon. Needless to say, my deer-gutting skills were never put to the test.

While Austin and I stood on Ninth Street, waiting for our burgers to cook, the conversation drifted to guns and dogs and the best way to get rid of squirrels. For some reason, the guys assumed (correctly) that I'd have opinions on these types of subjects. I could tell they sized me up as the kind of woman typified by the popular Gretchen Wilson song "Redneck Woman," which talks about not being a "high class broad" but rather someone who prefers to chug beer at honky-tonks.

Only in the most tangential way am I like this woman. Namely, if my marble lobby with a fountain was instead a front yard, I'd definitely stand barefoot in it with a baby on my hip. Nonetheless (since I was the closest thing to a redneck these gentlemen would ever meet), I unconsciously enhanced my drawl while Dominic sang, "Woo hoo, witchy woman," to a homeless lady badgering him for quarters.

On television, at least, Southern women are curvaceous coquettes—Daisy Duke, Elly May Clampett, and the Hee Haw Honeys—beautiful women who handle shotguns and curling irons with equal dexterity yet who still need family protection. Older Southern women, however, are straight talking and saintly, their lips dripping sage advice—the types of roles Dixie Carter and Jessica Tandy have played to perfection.

Southern men, on the other hand, are gentlemen, rednecks,

or affable fools. Characters like Forrest Gump, Gomer Pyle, and Jethro Bodine share a similar bumbling charm, whereas Bo and Luke Duke (who never *meant* no harm) predated the types of roles that Matthew McConaughey plays today. Rhett Butler, of course, was the quintessential gentleman, à la Robert E. Lee.

Our neighbors in New York used to leave their windows open during raucous sexual encounters, which caused David and me to wonder how much of their screaming (like cows stuck in a fence) was ecstasy and how much was porn-inspired affectation. Similarly, media portrayals have probably conditioned my own perceptions of Southern culture, speech patterns, and people. Even my own voice sounds weird to me, since I rarely hear similar accents, and I find myself pausing after a particularly long-drawled word. I'm suddenly self-conscious and wonder if I actually grew up pronouncing "might" with twenty-seven syllables, or if I just sound like a hick compared with Rene. When I go back South, however, and hear my dad say "ain't" instead of "aren't," it's almost like seeing an apparition, a puff of my past that had somehow been nudged over in my mind to make room for words like "plotzed" and "bagel."

One day I saw two guys kissing while waiting for the elevator on my floor.

"Hold the door!" I yelled when the doors opened and I still needed to drop a garbage bag down a nearby chute.

"Hello, *Survivor* T-shirt," they said, condescendingly checking out my garb as I slid in between them.

"Not just *Survivor*," I corrected. "*Survivor Australia* . . . the best *Survivor* so far."

The guys in the elevator noticed the signature of one of the contestants and asked, "Did Michael Stipe sign your shirt? Cool!"

"Not Stipe, Michael *Skupin*. The survivor who fell into the fire while cooking and had to be airlifted out while the other contestants watched teary eyed from the beach? The incident that made everyone momentarily forget the competition and reflect on their friendships before voting the next person off?"

"Sorry, don't watch it."

"How can you not?"

"Other things to do, I guess."

Awkward silence.

"Were you a part of the show or something?" They were appalled a person with good eyesight would buy a shirt like that. They were even more disturbed when I told them that David had actually tried out for *Survivor Africa* (then the next installment) while teaching ethics at Cornell Law School. We thought his job title plus his amazing pectorals would definitely catch the producer's eye in the three-minute audition video shot by students at the Cornell Film School. Alas, he was not destined to be known as "the Ultimate Survivor," "the Runner-up," or even "the Guy Who Stole the Beef Jerky." As a consolation, his students had given him the hideous autographed shirt. Which I grabbed to run out for ice cream, not expecting to get caught in the elevator with the fashion police.

After hearing the story, they said "Cool" in unison, which meant "lame." Then they proceeded to tell me they had looked at our apartment before settling on one down the hall.

"Hate to break it to you," they said, savoring the opportunity to break it to me. "Your apartment is nice, but ours is bigger."

I eyed them suspiciously. "Do you have two bedrooms, a loft, and a storage closet at the top of the stairs?"

"Sorry." They nodded. "Plus, we have an alcove connected to our bedroom."

"But I have new shag carpet."

"Ours is blue."

"Avocado-green appliances?"

They shook their heads and walked out the door, leaving me to explain to everyone in the lobby that I was sure my view was better. As I was standing there, I realized the inescapable truth that I had a stereotype of gay men in my head, and they probably had a stereotype of Southern women in theirs. What I found was that they fit perfectly into my mental image of them—attractive, funny, nice enough to hold the door for me, interested in the architectural curves of their apartment, and attentive to apparel. I'd just stepped into a *Will & Grace* episode.

But had we talked more, would I have fit into the stereotype they had of me?

Rene once asked me, "Does it hurt your feelings that some people think you're white trash?"

"Who thinks that?"

"For starters, this reader who suggests that you"—she looked down at some hate mail generated after a *City Paper* column and read aloud—"'move back to Tennessee where you can shop at Wal-Mart and hang out in your friends' trailer homes.'"

I grabbed the paper from her hands and realized Rene wouldn't know white trash unless they put a sofa on her front porch and started spitting tobacco into her potted plants. "Shopping at Wal-Mart doesn't make someone white trash."

Rene rolled her eyes. "Just unsympathetic to the plight of the underpaid employees."

"Do you know one person who's worked at Wal-Mart? David not only worked at Wal-Mart, he *sold guns* there."

I could tell that Rene was not impressed by my husband's level of sophistication. "You're making my point for me."

After all our moves, I've noticed the red/blue divide is most accurately characterized not by city versus country or lox versus grits, but rather by how people regard Wal-Mart. Admitting I shopped there while having coffee at someone's Philly home caused heated reactions—one asked, "Eww, why?" and another said, "It's too big, too overwhelming"—although they both shopped at the equally enormous liberal darling Ikea. When Daddy took us to Wal-Mart as kids, he'd pull into the football-field–size parking lot and say, "Wal-Mart will rule the world one day." And he didn't mean that as a criticism but rather in wide-eyed astonishment that a store headquartered in Bentonville, Arkansas, could attain such dominance.

"Wal-Mart paid better than David's first job," I said to Rene, who'd rather spend four times as much so she doesn't have to leave the shadows of the city skyscrapers.

"Which was?"

"Cleaning toilets at Big Lots."

"That doesn't exactly make Wal-Mart a champion of the poor," she said.

"Mother Teresa cornered that market," I said. "So I guess Wal-Mart just focused on selling things like cheap shampoo."

Wal-Marts in small-town America are now the hub of social activity—the front-of-the-store benches replaced the courthouse square as the place to sit and catch up with gossip. In fact, the quality of a town directly correlates to the size of its Wal-Mart. Nearby Camden, Tennessee, had a rinky-dink version that sat on the town's main thoroughfare like a missing front tooth— seeming to proclaim, "This town isn't sophisticated enough to deserve more." But when they finally decided to break ground on a Super Wal-Mart, it was such good news that my dad called to tell me.

Rene didn't share my appreciation of the store and would probably be embarrassed to know that David breaks out into the "Hallelujah Chorus" from Handel's *Messiah* when we drive by our small town's gleaming Wal-Mart on the hill.

I guess the difference is that we grew up believing that working at Wal-Mart, the gas station, or a fast-food joint was a privilege, not an embarrassment. In fact, a rite of passage for Southern kids rich and poor was donning a paper hat and upsizing people's fries. Part of the stereotyping of Southerners might have to do with the misunderstanding of the working class, the inability to comprehend people like my dad, who worried more about Lyme disease than carpal tunnel syndrome. Instead of loosening a tie when he got home like some people's fathers, my dad always sat on the porch and used masking tape to get the hundreds of tiny seed ticks off his arms that had lighted there during hours marking timber in the woods.

As I waited for my lunch from the food cart in the shadows of surrounding buildings, that memory seemed distant. The men waiting in line were pleased when my son told them he shot his first gun at the age of four (a BB gun my dad used to keep the squirrels off the porch), although I didn't tell them he's been so urbanized that he pointed out the window at a field of cows and exclaimed, "Look—horses!"

Perhaps I was overanalyzing the conversation; it was likely the men simply wanted a meaningless chat while Dominic sang and prepared the hot dogs. While talking to them, I guess I was keenly aware of the distance that separated me from home and slightly afraid other people would sense it too . . . that I'd somehow lost the essence of being Southern while hailing cabs and talking to doormen. Perhaps I cared way too much about a random conversation I happened to strike up with total strangers.

Or maybe that's what proved I was Southern to the core after all.

Wanna Coke?

I ONCE SOLD bicycles at a chichi New York sporting goods store called Paragon Athletics, filled with cutting-edge equipment for skiing, table tennis, golf, scuba diving, hockey, boxing, racquetball, and even lawn games. I blew most of my paychecks on their merchandise—Armani ski gear, Saucony footwear, Mountain Hardwear jackets—wanting to be a good steward of my employee discount. My manager Dan regularly lectured us about athletic knowledge, product presentation, and treating potential celebrity clientele like all our other customers—no gawking, asking for autographs, or acknowledgment of their identity. Nonchalance didn't come naturally for me; it was like trying to train my tongue away from a bad tooth. When Robert De Niro shuffled through our department, I was spellbound. When Martina Navratilova checked out the tennis racquets, I couldn't pry my eyes off her. When Calvin Broadus and his posse shopped for a jacket, I snooped around him like a D-O-double-G.

And so I tried to distract myself by organizing water bottles by height and color into a pretty impressive replication of the Manhattan skyline. The customers that wandered into the cycling department heard my accent and always wondered how on earth I wound up selling bikes on Broadway. Depending on my mood, I'd give them various answers: to make enough money to pay off my husband's law school debt, to attend NYU, or to see where Pace picante sauce was definitely not made. For some reason my Southern accent seemed to make my customers trust me more than the other salespeople. "Yes, sirree. These hundred-dollar spandex shorts are definitely what you're a-needin' for your biannual ten-minute bike ride in them there Hamptons."

I always knew Southerners didn't speak "standard English," whatever that was, and figured that somewhere in the Midwest, little children naturally spoke like television news anchors in perfectly nondescript English. My college communications professor advised me to lose the twang if I ever wanted to succeed in journalism—which was like asking me to give up my name, an essential part of my identity painful and awkward to alter. I had the feeling that if I could successfully give it up, something deep within me would necessarily change as well, that I might suddenly start drinking tea with my pinky finger extended, listening to NPR exclusively, and using phrases like "flyover country" to refer to my own hometown.

I learned that real newscasters have to train themselves painstakingly to speak standard, accentless English, no matter where they're from. It's not actually spoken in the Midwest or anywhere, for that matter. Instead, it's an accent taught only by linguistic coaches, based on a British accent spoken on the BBC but altered slightly to sound "authentically" American. This "standard" English is how the well-to-do people in the forties spoke—like in old movies—making standard English as conceptually concrete as the idea of the Easter Bunny. The editors of *The American Heritage Dictionary* qualify their definition of the term "standard English" by saying, "A form that is considered standard in one region may be nonstandard in another."[1]

When Supreme Court associate justice Potter Stewart struggled for a proper definition of obscenity, he ended the discussion by saying, "I know it when I see it." Like obscenity, standard English is impossible to define. But I had the feeling I'd know it if I heard it—and I definitely didn't hear it while growing up in West Tennessee. In spite of our accent—or perhaps because of it—history is rife with powerful Southern orators. For example, Georgia-born Martin Luther King Jr.'s spirited, sermonlike cadence helped make his "I have a dream" unforgettably powerful; Jesse Jackson, with the rise and fall of his South Carolinian voice, is certainly melodic if you can ignore what he's saying; and Arkansan Bill Clinton could deliver a speech like none other—having mastered the pitch and rhythm of a Baptist preacher, though, sadly, none of the conduct.

Almost every time a customer approached me with a question about cycling shoes or jerseys, they'd immediately be distracted by my accent. "I bet I know where you're from," they'd say triumphantly. "Texas."

Every single time, I'd smile like I'd never heard that and say, "Nope—I'm from Paris, Tennessee, home of the World's Biggest Fish Fry." This, of course, began many conversations about the variations of accents in the South and what exactly a fish fry was. This conversation played out dozens of times over the course of a day—I couldn't let people accuse me of being a Texan without setting them straight. Plus, it was a fast way to develop a relationship with each customer, an advantage when working on commission.

Once, however, the conversation didn't go as usual. A man came in who was participating in a triathlon, so I spent a great deal of time trying to outfit him with the requisite gear. After much conversation about gel seats, leather gloves, and the best chamois for spandex shorts, he looked at me and said, "I bet I can guess where you're from."

My coworkers rolled their eyes, but I smiled politely and said, "I bet you can't." He tossed his head back, thought for a moment, and then delivered his verdict with the confidence of a judge.

"You're from West Tennessee, within a thirty-mile radius of a little town called Dresden. But I also detect a tinge of mountain in there somewhere, so one or both of your parents are from Monteagle Mountain, around Chattanooga."

It was a slow day, so all my coworkers gathered around. "Is he right?" they asked, excited that they didn't have to hear about the fish fry again. I was astonished. Most people in New York are barely aware that Tennessee is a state, and I hadn't heard anyone mention Dresden—a town twenty-one miles away from Paris—since I left home.

We learned that my customer was not only a triathlete but also a modern-day Henry Higgins. He studied language patterns and rhythms of each American region so that he could usually pinpoint someone's hometown within fifty miles—making him very popular at parties. He explained to us that dialects are like tiny personal museums—records of oral traditions, passed down from one generation to the next.

For example, he said, people use telltale words that give

away their origins. People in Milwaukee and Boston might call water fountains "bubblers"—a term extinct in the rest of the nation. New Yorkers refer to the steps that lead up to the front door as a "stoop" (from the Dutch word *stoep*), a remnant from a time when New York was the Dutch colony of New Amsterdam.[2] Philadelphians are very combative about the proper term for the tiny chocolate hot-dog–shaped candy pieces strewn over ice cream. I call them sprinkles, but Rene's husband, Adam (a Philly native), calls them jimmies.

Bert Vaux, professor of linguistics at the University of Wisconsin in Milwaukee, says the way someone refers to a carbonated beverage is one of the most revealing ways to tell where they grew up. Most of the Midwest, Great Plains, and Pacific Northwest use "pop"; the Northeast, parts of the Midwest, and all of California use "soda"; and ever since Coca-Cola put its headquarters in Atlanta, virtually all Southern states, Texas, and parts of New Mexico[3] use "Coke." For example, you might overhear this exchange at dinner:

"Wanna Coke?"

"Sure. Gimme a Pepsi or a Sprite."

Linguists have determined that asking for Coke at parties in the Northeast might cause the host to deliver a substance that's not even a beverage.

One of the simplest foods—a sandwich made of a roll split lengthwise and filled with meats—causes the most complex language gymnastics. In New York City, it's called a *hero*; in Louisiana and parts of the South, it's a *poor boy*; in Maine, it's an *Italian sandwich*; in Philadelphia, it's a *hoagie*; and in parts of Connecticut, New York, and New Jersey, it's a *grinder*.

It might seem everyone would call it a *subway*, since there are more Subway restaurants in America than McDonald's and that infernal Jared won't stop bragging about his weight loss in commercials. The ubiquity of television sets, computers, and easily accessible highways would lead you to believe that everyone's accents would merge into a vapid yet unifying blandness.

Friends, for example, gave Jennifer Aniston more control over women's hairstyles than the pope had over contraceptive practices, and sarcastic half-completed sentences like "And I needed to know that be-*cause?*" became a part of the vernacular of the television savvy. People also began emphasizing odd words in sentences, such as "Could you *be* any ruder?" Linguists called it the "Chandler Bing-ing of America."[4]

Since American adults watch about thirty hours of television every week, will our accents eventually merge into one dull dialect?

Professor Vaux doesn't think so. "It's a misconception that dialects are dying out because of mass culture. Linguistic variations are just as rampant as ever. I believe that human beings have a strong need to identify with their own groups and distinguish themselves from others."[5] His online survey of regional speech demonstrates the distinct regional differences in pronunciation, idioms, and grammar found in pockets throughout the United States. Some believe the major dialects of the United States are actually becoming more dissimilar rather than more similar.

Our dialects express our complex cultural identities. Generally, we want to sound like the people we want to *be* like, not like people from other groups. My sister probably wants to sound like other suburban Nashville moms, my former pastor like other

Kentucky Pentecostal preachers, and my former professors like other instructors at NYU. According to Carmen Fought, associate professor of linguistics at Pitzer College, "This is why dialect differences will never disappear no matter how much TV we watch. We want to sound like the people around us and not like Ted Koppel.[6] (Unless we happen to be ambitious white male newscasters; then we might want to and probably will sound exactly like Ted Koppel.)" Of course, that same white male newscaster might be from a red state and be perfectly happy mimicking the drawl of Fox News's Shepard Smith, who hails from Holly Springs, Mississippi.

The New York City Marathon was the most exciting time of the year at Paragon. Every year, thirty thousand runners and two million spectators came to the city, with many sporting supply needs. Paragon hired forty translators—designated by various little flags on their vests—to assist the onslaught of foreign customers. The multilingual translators walked haughtily through our departments wearing as many as five national flags on their chests with more pride than veterans wear Purple Hearts. They looked at us regular employees with disdain, and we got the feeling they'd rather be hanging out at the UN getting autographs than helping a sporting goods store sell energy bars. As a joke, our mechanic Desmond made a little Confederate flag and secretly pinned it on my polyester vest before I came into work one morning. He gave himself away by leaving a large thumbprint of grease on the back and by giggling nervously behind the glove display when I put it on.

"You're just as good as them." Desmond's voice piped out from behind the gloves. "You can translate redneck into Yankee."

No matter how many languages were being spoken in Paragon at any given moment, the only speech pattern guaranteed to raise eyebrows was the drawl. Once Southerners were detected, the sales associates pointed them up to my floor, where we'd hang out and perform verbal tricks for bystanders for beef jerky and fried chicken legs—"Say 'pen' for us, okay? And 'kite' just one more time?"

Usually, the Southern customers would buy something from cycling just to be polite. "Look, Bill. They have handlebar tape! Just what we're a-needin' for the marathon."

My little Confederate flag drew lots of laughs before my manager yanked it off my chest and unceremoniously tossed it in the trash can. For a few brief moments, though, I was not merely a salesperson but an ambassador. I walked through the store with my head held high, overcoming the cultural divide, one jogger at a time.

The Real Curse of the Jade Scorpion

DURING MY SHORT stint as a liberal, David and I watched several Woody Allen flicks—we laughed at *The Purple Rose of Cairo*, applauded *Hannah and Her Sisters,* and fidgeted uncomfortably through *Husbands and Wives*. After the final credits, we discussed the underlying themes, teased out subtle meanings of the symbolism, and felt quite heady with the intoxication of budding romance.

You've probably already guessed what it took me several months and a wedding to finally comprehend: David's whole dating persona was a ruse. Not only did he pretend to love Woody Allen flicks, he also faked disdain for sports. Only later did I realize he was involved in fantasy football and baseball leagues, had a great three-point shot that he showed off in his weekly basketball games, and played all-night paintball games with friends.

It took me a while to catch on, however, to his cinematic preferences . . . with slips of the tongue, contradicting statements, and . . . well, the fact he camped out with hundreds of other blow-'em-up enthusiasts for the premiere of Will Smith's blockbuster *Independence Day*. I joined him at the Ziegfeld Theater in Manhattan, hours before the movie began, and was shocked to see we'd been beaten there by a hundred guys even geekier than we were, dressed as aliens and having pizza delivered to their part of the line. And they were all males. When I made this observation to David, he said, "Are you kidding me? They're all just saving a space for their supermodel girlfriends. I'm sure Tyra Banks will be here any minute."

After the ring was securely on my finger, he never voluntarily watched another Woody Allen movie again. I managed to drag him to *Everyone Says I Love You* and *Small Time Crooks*, which he enjoyed well enough. But *The Curse of the Jade Scorpion* was the nail in my Woody Allen coffin, and we are currently doomed to watch movies involving muscular male heroes (CIA agents, marines, or presidents) risking everything they hold dear to save the planet from aliens, tidal waves, or deadly viral strains. The higher the body count, the better. In fact, when we moved to Philadelphia, David's main complaint was that all the Ritz movie theaters played flicks heavy on the dialogue and light on the body bags. If he wanted to see the latest blockbuster, he had to drive to New Jersey because the theaters within walking distance were busy with back-to-back showings of *Brokeback Mountain*.

Barely half of conservatives describe themselves as "intellectual," but 75 percent of liberals do.[1] Writer David Brooks pointed out that people in the red states "don't complain that Woody Allen isn't as funny as he used to be, because they never thought he was funny." Our closest circle of friends in Kentucky were educated folk who practiced law, owned hotels, and could pick a winning horse at Keeneland based on how it bucked in the starting gate. But in all the years we've been friends, we've never had a conversation about the latest piece in *The New Yorker*, how to survive in a postmodern society, or how to pro- actively create paradigm shifts. In fact, the most heated discus- sions were usually reserved for the basketball courts. It's not that these people were less intelligent than their blue state counter- parts, but wearing intelligence on your sleeve is just not done down there.

This reticence is not present in the North, where people re- gale you with a *Reader's Digest* version of their résumés within minutes of introduction and the unabridged version if you're not adept at excusing yourself for a cocktail. One woman—who was wearing the shirt equivalent of a bikini top while picking up her kindergartner from school—told me other women didn't like her because she was gorgeous, intelligent, and confident in her sexuality. David noticed in his circles that if someone's opinion was questioned, they'd recite their list of accomplishments in- stead of discussing the issue at hand. "How can you question me? I am the son of Latvian immigrants and have written thirty arti- cles about this very subject for . . ."

I've noticed this behavior manifests itself in the way people raise their kids. If Camille came home and said, "I am the smartest kid in my whole class," I would probably answer with something like "There's no need to put down everyone in your class," whereas Rene would probably tell her son, "Yes, Ethan, you're a smart boy, and you can do anything you set your mind to." Noting this phenomenon, David Brooks writes, "If I had to describe the differences between the two sensibilities in a single phrase, it would be conception of the self. In Red America the self is small. People declare in a million ways, 'I am normal. Nobody is better, nobody is worse. I am humble before God.' In Blue America the self is more commonly large. People say in a million ways, 'I am special. I have carved out my own unique way of life. I am independent. I make up my own mind.'"[2]

This refusal to elevate oneself above others—intellectually or otherwise—may help exacerbate the stereotype that conservatives are idiots, as typified by the front page of Britain's *Daily Mirror* screaming, "How Can 59,054,087 People Be So DUMB?" Additionally, after Bush beat Al Gore in 2000, a fake IQ chart went around the Internet faster than a Paris Hilton home video, appearing in hundreds of liberal blogs like the Daily Kos and even in the August edition of *The Economist*. The hoax was called "States with Higher IQ Vote Democrat" and listed states by their supposed levels of intelligence—the Einsteinian blue states outscoring the knuckle-dragging red states by enormous gaps. Connecticut was listed at the top of the chart at 113 (followed by fifteen more blue states). The bottom half of the chart were all red states, with Mississippi scoring a mere 85 points. *The Economist* later had to publish this retraction: "Last week we published a list that purported to show the IQs of states voting for George Bush and Al Gore in 2000. Alas, we were the victim of a hoax: no such data exists." Immediately following Bush's victory over Kerry, this fictitious table spread over the Internet again.

Rene's husband, Adam, was a victim of the ruse. One night at dinner, we were arguing about the so-called inadequacies of my Land Rover. (He is in the automotive business and has a definite opinion on what kinds of cars and trucks people should purchase—primarily the ones in his dealership.) Finally he blew me off by saying I couldn't help my ignorant SUV-buying decisions because of my heritage. "It's true. Blue states are statistically smarter," he said. "I'm not just making this up. My brother sent me an e-mail about it. Said Mississippi was barely more intelligent, on average, than this dinner plate."

"Don't insult my dinner plate," Rene said, serving perfectly baked chicken next to buttered rolls and corn. I instantly felt compassion for Adam and almost didn't want to point out the deception. After all, being gullible enough to fall for a hoax that's designed to make you feel smarter might be the apex of pride and arrogance . . . dare I call it inherently stupid? Adam is my friend, I thought. I certainly didn't want to embarrass him in front of his children. Instead, I leaned in close to him and whispered, letting the bomb drop quietly. He'd been duped, the chart was a trick, I explained, trying to soften the blow by allowing him to have all the dark meat on the platter.

"Those charts might've been fakes, but you can't fool me. I saw *Deliverance*," he said, shoveling food into his mouth. I figured Adam's recrimination probably would come much later, when he was lying in bed in the stillness of the night, reflecting on the day's events. I hoped he wouldn't be too hard on himself. I decided to eat quickly and leave him so as not to embarrass him further. When I announced I was leaving, he said, "Hope your Land Rover starts."

But this wasn't the first time liberals had fallen for a Republicans-are-idiots–type hoax. In 2001, some pranksters issued a fake press release from the Lovenstein Institute—a nonexistent organization purportedly based in Scranton, Pennsylvania—that claimed President Bush had the lowest presidential IQ in the past fifty years. It assigned President Clinton double the intelligence quotient of George H. W. Bush—who somehow managed to graduate Phi Beta Kappa in two and a half years from Yale in spite of his mental inadequacies—and gave President George W. Bush the lowest IQ, 91. The press release was an obvious spoof, since all the Democrats ranked exceptionally high and the Republicans were all moderate or average. But that wasn't enough to tip off blue state geniuses like Garry Trudeau. He was so certain it was true he wrote it into his *Doonesbury* strip.[3] London's *The Guardian* and New Zealand's *Southland Times* both ran the "Presidential IQ" tale as a factual item,[4] and it was only reported later by the Associated Press and *U.S. News & World Report* to be a hoax.

The liberals were easily taken in by the hoaxes because they purportedly confirm what they already believe in their hearts—conservatives have to be morons to believe what they do. Howell Raines, the former executive editor of the *New York Times*, succinctly demonstrated this when he asked, "Does anyone in America doubt that Kerry has a higher IQ than Bush? I'm sure the candidates' SATs and college transcripts would put Kerry far ahead."

It was hard to tell, since Kerry refused to authorize the release of his transcripts until the June after he lost the election. What they revealed was surprising—Kerry's four-year average was on par with President Bush's,[5] and military tests put Bush slightly ahead intellectually. This was surprising, rather, to everyone but red staters, who don't see a refusal to broadcast academic achievements as a sign of mental weakness. It's simply impolite in the South to brag—of your intellect or otherwise—and President Bush is the perfect example of this Southern reserve. His two degrees—one from Yale and the other from Harvard—didn't play well in Texas where they're more likely to judge you by the size of your belt buckle. An article in *The American Conservative* stated, "In the president's lone losing race, his 1978 run for Congress from West Texas, the victor stressed Bush's two Ivy League degrees. Bush resolved never to allow himself to be outdumbed again. And the Democrats haven't outsmarted him since."[6]

During our marriage, I've spent untold hours with David's law firm colleagues. Some of these individuals were blindingly brilliant. They had performed well in every academic setting, could write legal briefs that literally made you cry (moved by emotion, not boredom), and won multimillion-dollar lawsuits with ease. But there are intelligent lawyers all over America. What made these individuals special? You could not tell they were smart. They were regular folks who sometimes spoke with a twang and never, ever led anyone to believe they had any intellectual gifts whatsoever. It was always better to be "misunderestimated." In the middle of the election season, David answered the thousandth allegation that George Bush was an idiot: "You know who Bush reminds me of? A lawyer from Kentucky who would win millions in lawsuits against the Northeast's best law firms and then—hours after the jury returned its verdict—tip back a glass of beer, smile, and say, 'You know, I think that New York lawyer mighta thought I was dumb.'"

I guess I shouldn't be too hard on the liberals who were

taken in by the fake IQ reports. We can all be fooled. After all, I was totally duped by David's dating persona. At the time, I loathed my little conservative college and simply wanted to discuss the cinematic works of a man who later would marry his own daughter. Was that too much to ask? When a friend at Lipscomb asked what I liked about Woody Allen films, I went into great detail about satire and humor. She looked at me blankly, then said, "I guess I just don't get it." I took that to mean I was smarter than she was, that she would rather "sing and be happy" than explore the deeper meanings of life, that she was content to skirt by on life's trivialities. That's the thing about condescension. You don't have to actually be smarter than others to use it as a conversational tool; you must just have the willingness to elevate yourself while putting down others. This may not be the healthiest way to deal with other people, but I've found it's a lot easier than actually taking a hard look at oneself. Now, pass the popcorn.

Country

America is the country where you can buy a lifetime
supply of aspirin for one dollar and use it up in two weeks.
—*John Barrymore, Philadelphia actor*

I have no further use for America. I wouldn't go back
there if Jesus Christ was President.
—*Charlie Chaplin*

The Exhausted American

MY NEW YEAR'S resolution was to be the person who *had* the chewing gum, mints, and Kleenexes instead of the person constantly asking for them. Maybe because my purse isn't made by Samsonite—or brimming with diaper wipes, baby Tylenol, tweezers, and Goldfish crackers—I always feel ill prepared as a mother. The other day, I was meeting some women for coffee when one of them noticed a flat tire. Lo and behold, someone pulled Fix-A-Flat out of her handbag. I felt so inadequate. Three decades of misplaced keys, lost credit cards, and forgotten birthdays convinced me that this year was the year I would metamorphose from an irresponsible twentysomething who gets by on charm to a mature thirtysomething who Has It All Together.

My resolution was quickly broken when I went nervously to see my daughter sing at her first talent show. Since she'd never sung in front of anyone publicly, stage fright was as inevitable as someone choosing to sing a Whitney Houston song. I was worried she'd freeze or run crying offstage. So the night before the show, I devised a strategy. First, I dragged her to our building lobby and made her sing to our doorman Ed, using his pen as a microphone. Several tenants and even the Chinese deliveryman applauded her effort, so then we were off to the twentieth-floor fire escape overlooking Chestnut Street. From there she sang, "My country, 'tis of thee, sweet land of liberty . . ." at the top of her lungs to the pedestrians walking below, while she held the flag across her chest and pretended she was singing in the auditorium of her school. By the time David walked her to school the next morning, she was ready.

But I wasn't. Around eleven o'clock, David, Austin, and I were walking to the school auditorium when I realized I'd left her one prop—the flag—at home. She was scheduled to perform at 11:20, after the electric guitar riff and before the Mariah Carey power ballad. I had exactly nineteen minutes.

I started to run.

It was 91 degrees, and I'd worn a skirt—not the best attire for dodging coffee carts and jumping over the homeless. I'd really messed up this time. In my lifetime, I've had my phone service turned off twice due to forgotten bills, bounced more checks than MC Hammer, and even accidentally set my house on fire. I can barely take care of myself, I thought. How am I supposed to keep track of a family? But mostly I was thinking about an offhand comment a parent had made as my husband dropped my daughter off at school that morning: "I hope no one boos her song because it's patriotic."

I hadn't thought of that. There's obvious political tension at Camille's Philadelphia public school. Some parents drove cars with bumper stickers like "The Only Thing Bush Fixes . . . Are Elections" and "The Christian Right Is Neither." So a song proclaiming America belongs to God very well might not have drawn the standing ovation she deserved. In fact, a song indicating America was anything but stealing the world's oil so we can drive SUVs over the bodies of foreigners would've been poorly received in Philadelphia.

It wasn't always so. Immediately after the September 11 attacks, Americans of both regions stood unanimous in their reactions to the event. More than four-fifths of Americans supported a military response against terror and more than three-fifths said they supported a military response even if it meant thousands of U.S. casualties. There were no significant discrepancies between red state and blue state Americans.[1]

American flags were stuck on the bumpers of SUVs, minivans, and taxicabs across America. Flags were embroidered on the uniforms of athletes and were draped reverently from front porches everywhere. And then something happened. The immediate surge of patriotism passed like a bad case of the flu, and most people in the blue areas were glad to be cured of it.

Susan Sontag spoke of the hijackers and asked, "Where is the acknowledgment that this was not a 'cowardly' attack on 'civilization' or 'liberty' or 'humanity' or 'the free world,' but an attack on the world's self-proclaimed superpower, undertaken as a consequence of specific American alliances and actions?"[2] Additionally, a piece in *The Nation* stated that the American flag stood for "jingoism and vengeance and war."[3] In other words, while America prepared itself for a "new kind of war," we also were encountering a new kind of peace protester—those who believed American foreign policy was so evil we deserved our passenger airliners to be hijacked and used as missiles against our populace. Some colleges even banned American flags from students' dorm rooms, citing a policy outlawing "harassing or intimidating" visual materials[4] as they fitfully prepared their auditoriums for viewing *Fahrenheit 9/11*.

Not to be outdone in the area of absurdity, the Reverend Jerry Falwell came out with his own reaction to events: "I really believe that the pagans, and the abortionists, and the feminists, and the gays and the lesbians who are actively trying to make that an alternative lifestyle, the ACLU, People for the American Way—all of them who have tried to secularize America—I point the finger in their face and say 'You helped this happen.' "[5]

Of course Americans were outraged that we were being blamed for the 9/11 attacks by both liberals (who said we were a nation of arrogant patriots) and conservatives (who said we were a nation of arrogant sinners).

What it means to be either is hotly contested. In the South, people tend to be very patriotic, especially after 9/11. For example, University of Kentucky football games kicked off with a rendition of Lee Greenwood's "God Bless the USA," while a montage of American soldiers in action played on the jumbo screen. Then followed the singing of the national anthem (prompting all the men to remove their ball caps), topped off by the climactic flyover of Black Hawk helicopters from 101st Airborne. Churches held services and picnics to honor the families of soldiers, and Wal-Mart hung photographs of soldiers from the community on their front walls.

But in Philadelphia I constantly saw bumper stickers that read "Support Our Troops—Bring Them Home" or "Peace *Is* Patriotic." And while it's certainly possible to support the troops without supporting the war, this sometimes manifests in very unpalatable ways. Probably the most brazen example was played out at a Pennsylvania funeral of a marine killed in Iraq, where Lieutenant Governor Catherine Baker Knoll showed up late and uninvited. She sat down in a pew next to a family member during Communion and asked, "Who are you?" Now, there are many things you should never say at a funeral. You should never call "shotgun" on the parking space of the deceased, say to someone, "You look like you've seen a ghost," or yell, "I object!" during the eulogy. But of all the preposterous things to say at a funeral, the lieutenant governor of Pennsylvania managed to top them all. After determining the person sitting beside her was the soldier's aunt, she took out one of her business cards, handed it to the grieving woman, and assured her "our government" is against the war.[6] Then she went out to a film crew and expressed her condolences on television.

There was little outcry over this among my liberal friends. To them, the war is so egregious that they would've thought the lieutenant governor's comments would actually be comforting to the family. The media rarely features any families who support the war, choosing rather to focus on the vocal parents who become peace protesters and march in Washington after their family members enlist, or tragically die, in the fight against terror. They rarely if ever show the faces of proud, grief-stricken families who believe freedom is not only worth fighting for but also worth dying for. My liberal friends have a mantra—"Bush lied, people died"—that they stick on any vehicle they own or into any conversation they may be having.

While I believe that statement is less historically accurate than a typical episode of *The Flintstones*, I'm the first to admit my own patriotism is based on a lie. Well, that and a piece of beef.

My dad's family lived well below the poverty line but wouldn't take a cent of money from the state. There was no food in his house and no money for school lunch. So every day he pretended to go home for lunch, sat behind a tree while watching the kids in the cafeteria through a window, and returned with a toothpick in his mouth as if he'd just devoured a feast. By the time he was fifteen, he had dropped out of high school six times. One day he found a military enlistment card in a magazine, lied about his age on the form, and dropped it in the post office box. Almost immediately the United States military came calling, and his mom ran them off, one branch of service at a time. The recruiters for the army, the navy, and the air force were no match for Cleo Anderson's belief that her fifteen-year-old boy shouldn't be a soldier. But by the time the Marine Corps recruiter showed up on the doorstep of their three-room home, her resolve had worn thin. "I'm not gonna stop ya if you're determined to leave," she said. The recruiter changed Dad's name, altered his birthday to make him older, and shipped him to Parris Island. On the first day of basic training, they served steak in the mess hall, and he felt full for the first time in his life.

That rib eye is probably responsible for my patriotism today. In his three years of service, the kid who'd never stepped foot off the mountain visited twenty-eight countries. He grew up to be a great father to three little girls, one of whom always thought she detected tears in his eyes whenever the national anthem was played.

My family sang patriotic songs in church, at the ballpark, and around the piano in the living room. To be honest, I'd never thought hard about the lyrics to "America" before Camille's talent show. I'd helped her select it because the "let freedom ring" part fit in nicely with the Liberty Bell motif, and it was brief enough for her to memorize.

However, the whole performance was about to be ruined because I'd forgotten the flag.

I broke into a full sweat as I ran through Washington Square Park, but my mind raced with resentment over all the anti-American sentiment at the school. I, for one, don't care if the French hate us. (As Senator Kit Bond said, "Going to the war without France is like going deer hunting without an accordion.") But the anti-American sentiment from condescending Americans is what annoyed me. It's like I had to be "ironic" in my appreciation of a country that deposed Saddam Hussein, a genocidal maniac whose regime was responsible for a million brutal deaths—including killing tens of thousands of women and children through his ethnic cleansing.

By the time I finally made it to my apartment (11:07), I was disenchanted, gasping for air, and trying not to pass out. I grabbed the flag but noticed it wasn't very substantial—in fact, it was fastened with two tiny staples to a small wooden rod. When I ran, I yanked it around too much, so I held it upright to keep it as motionless as possible.

I had to will myself to take each step. It was nine minutes past eleven and I was running out of steam. Then a weird thing happened. A man on the street started clapping. Then another. With each step I willed myself to make, more and more people began clapping. I began looking for hidden cameras and Ashton Kutcher. What was going on?

I caught a glimpse of my reflection as I passed a building's window. There I was, running through the city holding an American flag high above my head, looking positively Olympian. Suddenly people all over the sidewalks were turning to encourage me. It suddenly dawned on me. In a city with daily activities to raise money for medical research or political causes, they thought I was doing some sort of charitable race. One man said, "Go, America!" I'm not sure what kind of race would have runners wearing skirts and shades, but in Philadelphia it's hard to look weirder than your surroundings. The fact I was drenched in sweat, panting for air, and staggering on the edge of passing out probably led them to believe I wasn't doing this for fun, that there had to be some sort of cause behind it.

It was a very odd situation. On one hand, I was touched by their obvious goodwill toward our country and me. But on the other hand, I—just a mom with short-term memory problems—didn't deserve their applause.

I couldn't very well stop and explain myself. I was rapidly running out of time and could barely breathe. Unsure of what exactly to do, I decided simply to enjoy it. All the way to my daughter's school, I smiled and waved like a beauty queen on a float to construction workers, a mailman, and a lady buying a newspaper, all who were under the impression they were encouraging an exhausted American.

And, after all the cynicism I'd been around, they were right.

Might as Well Delete "Indivisible" Too

FINDING A GOOD school is like falling in love. So when Camille got accepted into a school one block from our apartment, we were flush with excitement. We'd always wanted to raise our children bilingually but had been plagued with the pesky inconvenience of not knowing another language ourselves. When the children were young, David and I trudged out into the snow every Tuesday to our Spanish classes but kept making mistakes. During the holidays, for example, I inadvertently wished people a "Happy new anus," and then apologized by saying something like "Please forgive me, I'm so pregnant." Since this new school had a complete Spanish immersion program, we were well on our way to raising our own Mexican vacation tour guide.

The way immersion works is simple. The teachers conduct all their instruction in Spanish, and the children pick it up as naturally as they picked up English. In fact, they don't even introduce English until the third grade, making Spanish immersion an ambitious but rewarding experience. We didn't take it lightly. And since Camille was already in a great public school (which also taught Mandarin Chinese every day), we felt like philanderers. In fact, Rene and I didn't tell anyone we'd filled out an application for the school until we knew our kids had been accepted, covertly researching the benefits of bilingual education and slipping into the school's open house under the darkness of night.

It seemed like a perfect match in the way that online dating profiles can mislead you into believing you've found your soul mate even before you pick up the phone. I should've known something was askew when I went on a tour of the school and saw an entire wall of construction paper artwork maligning the president. I stopped momentarily and read the children's writing: "John Kerry is an honorable soldier, unlike George W."; "America hates George Bush because he is a liar"; "George Bush hates minorities." Sometimes, when you're falling in love, you overlook the flaws. After all, it was a public school. Even if the kids were all little Michael Moores, at least the teachers had to be fair and nonpartisan, we thought.

When we went to back-to-school night, there were more hints of problems to come. One of the first people to speak was the chair of the diversity committee, who got up and explained how much work she had to do. (Even though the room was filled with Egyptians, Africans, Asians, and even two Southerners, there's never enough diversity for a diversity committee.) Then the principal got up and explained the first-grade choir was going to sing the national anthem in Spanish at a United Nations gala celebrating their anniversary. David started squeezing my hand. Like Spider-Man's Spidey sense warns him of trouble, David has a conservative wince that detects liberal speak. On the wall a sign read: "At 'Public School X'" (not named to protect the guilty), "we use Public School X words."

"I wonder what those words are?" I whispered.

"Probably an oath to the Democratic Party," David replied.

Nevertheless, we ignored the warning signs and forged ahead with our new relationship with the school. We struggled with the homework, which came with Spanish instructions, and I could tell Camille was exhausted after each day.

One afternoon, when we were talking about how her day went, she burst into tears. When they were reciting the Pledge of Allegiance, she had unknowingly walked into the line of fire.

"We're not allowed to say 'under God' here," three boys had admonished her in front of the class, to her great embarrassment.

Usually when I tell people my husband is a lawyer, they ask about car accidents or wills. So when I explain he's a constitutional lawyer who specializes in freedom of speech issues, their eyes glaze over with the uninterest that comes from not getting free legal advice. This time, however, David's expertise came in handy. He sat Camille in his lap and explained that this country was founded on freedom of religion (ironically, the school sits in the shadow of Independence Hall, where the Constitution and Declaration of Independence were signed) and that she could say "under God" if she wanted to.

"But even the principal won't say it," she explained. "Should I?"

David and I exchanged glances. Since we had chosen to live in this blue city, we were accustomed to going against the flow. However, we weren't willing to make our kids into some sort of cultural martyrs, so we told her she could do whatever she felt was right.

When I talked to the principal about their policy, she began by explaining their general philosophies. When they pick out their textbooks, for example, they are very careful to make sure all kinds of people are represented in the illustrations. There's nothing wrong with a book that features only blond-haired, blue-eyed kids, she told me, except that it implies there's something wrong if you aren't. Sometimes in textbooks, what is not being said is just as important as what is being said, she explained, and it's very important to make sure all students are represented. Similarly, they had decided to eliminate the phrase "under God" from the pledge because they didn't want to make students who don't believe in God feel uncomfortable.

After much soul searching, Camille decided to say "under God" quickly and quietly so no one else could hear her. But when I picked her up from school the next day, she was still afraid of being punished. The next day, Camille's teacher called me and had me come to school to visit Camille because she was acting so gloomy. With her homework, she brought home a sheet that read: "I am feeling . . ." Under that phrase were dozens of teddy bears with different expressions—joy, surprise, anger, confusion. Camille had colored in the one that read "sad." She asked all types of questions: Do the people at my school hate God? Do they dislike Christians? Are they trying to make me not believe in God?

In other words, the decision to remove "under God" from the pledge wasn't making *everyone* feel comfortable, nor was it designed to. Instead, it was pure politics, designed to make *cer-*

tain types of students comfortable—namely the ones who held political beliefs deemed "acceptable" by the school board. On the intercom every morning, a disclaimer was read: "We are about to say the Pledge of Allegiance. If you do not wish to say the pledge, you are not being compelled to say it. But we ask all students to stand out of respect."

So students who object to "under God" already have the right not to *say* it, but the board thought they shouldn't even have to *hear* it. In other words, the board's editing of the pledge reflected the real travesty here—that they believe students with minority viewpoints are weaker minded and need more protection than other students. The principal betrayed this on the phone when she told me that students holding minority viewpoints who did not want to say "under God" might not be able to resist the pressure to join in (even in spite of the daily disclaimer). She assured me Camille could say it by squeezing it in quickly between the words "nation" and "indivisible." However, when I turned the tables and said my daughter might feel compelled *not* to say "under God" as everyone skips it, her only response was to assure me Camille was sophisticated enough to handle it.

Of course, the original pledge didn't have the phrase in it at all—it was added in 1954 by a nearly unanimous vote of both Republican and Democratic Congress members. An elementary school principal trading the democratically decided pledge for the original version is like disregarding the First Amendment because it wasn't in the original Constitution.

It also does a disservice to those with minority viewpoints in other ways too—most notably by failing to equip them to face the real world of political debate and compromise. If principals and professors are offended by a law, they should use the democratic process to seek change; they should not simply ignore the law to follow their own preferred course.

The fact is, people will be offended in a multicultural society. I was offended by Clinton's entire presidency. However, I didn't arbitrarily lump myself in a group of like-minded people and pretend he wasn't president. Instead, I tried to elect someone who better reflected my views by wearing campaign stickers, writing newspaper articles, and resisting the voter registration people who urged me to name my next child Kerry.

Similarly, if the school believed the Pledge of Allegiance to be antiquated, then the board members had the right to petition their congressmen, campaign for a candidate who shares their views, or make a human pyramid of protest outside the White House with Cindy Sheehan. However, making their political statement using my six-year-old was an insidious abuse of power, one that tax dollars shouldn't have had to subsidize.

According to their Web site, the school attempts to teach the "values of our pluralistic democracy." I could only hope that my daughter didn't know enough Spanish to understand the class about ignoring opposing viewpoints, isolating themselves in their own little world, and hoping everything turns out okay.

But I guess they'd already taught that lesson. Sometimes what you don't say is even more important than what you do.

Turning Tables

I USED TO wait tables at a Nashville restaurant called Dalt's, which was like every other fern bar in the city except that it was conveniently located near Belle Meade—the part of town with Greek Revival mansions and Jaguars in the driveways. Dalt's was a classic American diner—huge burgers, malted shakes, and great fries—but with enough diversity in our menu to keep our base of wealthy customers loyal.

At the beginning of my stint, I didn't know much about waitressing unless the customer was ordering something smothered, covered, or scattered. In other words, I did have previous experience, but the Huddle House in Paris hadn't taught me how to read a wine list. Although I tried to make up for my total ineptitude with a heapin' helpin' of charm, my manager gave me the fewest number of tables—the ones next to the bathroom that were full only on the weekend after all the booths were taken. But even with decreased responsibility, I still struggled with basics. I served cork remnants in the wine, and I wasn't familiar with any of the cocktails. ("I'm sorry, sir, but propositioning me for sex on the beach will *not* get your quesadillas here faster.") While most servers loved orders with alcohol—larger bills and tips—I had to write down every detail of each drink. The customer invariably rattled off her order faster than her own name. "Pardon me, ma'am, did you want that Belvedere up, dry and dirty, two olives and one onion in an ice-cold glass stirred or shaken?" Frequently, people tried to show off in front of their friends: "I'll have an Irish whiskey single-barrel, nothing younger than a twenty-year, peaty, not too smoky." Or when ordering champagne, they clarified that it "must be an artisanal, single vineyard, off-dry, blanc de blanc and I won't drink any vintage but 1996." Complicating matters even further, Dalt's served over a hundred varieties of beer. About twice a day, customers would ask about our selection, and I'd nervously start down my alphabetical list: "Amstel Light, Asahi, Bass, Beck's, Dos Equis, Foster's, Guinness, Heineken, Killian's Irish Red . . ." Their eyes glazed over by the time I reached Michelob, while the eyes of other patrons needing attention bored holes into my back. Nine times out of ten—after listening to the whole list— the customer would lean back, look up at the ceiling, and say, "Why don't ya just bring me a Bud?" like the thought had just occurred to him.

Since I didn't get much practice eating in nice restaurants in Paris, I was also ignorant of basic menu details. I'd never eaten a fajita, so I didn't know to bring all the requisite accompaniments (tortillas, refried beans, Mexican rice, pico de gallo, lettuce, sour cream, and guacamole) with the dramatically smoking skillets. I remember being surprised that people kept ordering platters of meat—this was before the Atkins diet became popular—and suspicious foods called garden burgers or turkey burgers. I almost got fired when I got the nonbeef patties mixed up, which resulted in an overdramatic vegetarian dry-heaving in the aisle.

After a few months, I did finally get the hang of some things. I learned to up-sell ("Would you like the artichoke dip while you wait, or are you saving room for our famous rock slide pie?"). And I quickly learned what it meant to be "in the weeds"—to be overcome and behind with the customers. I learned that a table's "turn" was one cycle of seating, serving, and clearing a group of people at a table—obviously, the more tables you turn per night, the more money you make. One couple's lingering romantically over coffee at lunch could be the difference between a waitress's rent being paid or not.

I also attained the ability every server eventually perfects— stereotyping. I could take one look at my customers and know if they were ostentatious spenders (pointing at the most expensive wine on the menu to avoid having to pronounce the name), the hardworking wealthy (spending lots of money but with discretion), the coupon users (forgetting to tip on the whole bill), the special occasionists (rarely going out but ordering all the courses when they do), and the wish-they-were-younger group of men (drinking four rounds of "whatever's on tap" and tipping way too much to prove they had money to burn).

Dalt's, however, had an extra category of customer who made the job more interesting and sometimes more profitable— the country music star. On occasion, a celebrity stopped by, and we all begged the hostess to seat him in our section. Other than an inordinate number of waitstaff hovering around making sure their tea glasses were full, the country stars blended in pretty well. So well, in fact, that once, after a mild-mannered guy in a ball cap tipped me handsomely on his credit card, I looked at the receipt and was surprised to be saying, "Thank you, Mr. . . . Gill."

Vince Gill, like many other country musicians, seems to take pride in being just like everyone else. Mark Miller, the lead singer of Sawyer Brown who stopped by pretty regularly for Dalt's Key lime pie, has a quote on his Web site which sums up this mentality: "I ain't first class and I ain't white trash—that's who I am, and who our fans are. . . . The people who shop at Wal-Mart . . . we're proud that we are those people." This down-home touch is evident in their accessibility to their fans. Country music even has an annual event specifically for the fans—the Fan Fair—which includes thirty hours of live music and endless autograph-signing sessions.

And those country fans are not easily defined. The old joke about what you get when you play a country song backward—your house, your car, your wife, and your dog back—suggests this genre appeals only to those who wear Carhartt and chew tobacco. At Harvard, however, David learned otherwise. He used to watch County Music Television while studying because it reminded him of home. This caused his Ivy League friends to mock him endlessly, until one day he challenged them. "You watch the next video that comes on the television. If you don't like it, then at least you'll be an informed critic."

One accepted the bet, settled in on the couch, and didn't even try to hide the condescending smirk on her face. The next song that came on was quintessentially country—a sappy song about a man and his dog called "Feed Jake" by the Pirates of the Mississippi. By the end of the song, at least one person was dead, another had to assume pet care responsibilities, and David's friend was crying hot, wet tears on the couch. She never ridiculed him again.

One Harvard convert does not create a movement, so it was hardly surprising that the decision to hold the 39th Annual Country Music Awards in—of all places—New York City dismayed Nashvillians and puzzled New Yorkers. Some country musicians have been known to loathe the Big Apple—just listen to the title of Buck Owens's immortal "I Wouldn't Live in New York City (If They Gave Me the Whole Dang Town)."

Acting out in frustration, one of Nashville's most popular radio hosts called random New Yorkers out of the phone book every morning to ask them basic questions about the genre: "Name one country musician or song." Usually they couldn't come up with anyone, except for the universally adored Dolly Parton. Some even took pride in their ignorance, fanning the flames of Tennessee resentment even more.

New Yorkers were hardly thrilled with their new guests. It's obvious you can't spell "Grand Ole Opry" without the GOP, and New Yorkers were already irritated about having to play host to the Republican convention. The city collectively groaned when Mayor Bloomberg donned a white Stetson to announce the historic move of the ceremony while playing a video of him pretending to strum a guitar. He then referred to Tim McGraw as "Tom" and Shania Twain as "Shanaga." Reporters at the press conference mistakenly addressed Kix Brooks (of the country music duo Brooks & Dunn) as "Mr. Dunn." When one reporter asked the mayor to name his favorite country song, he couldn't name even one.

The press had a field day with this clash of cultures. Commenting on the bizarre press conference, the New York *Daily News* declared, "Yee-huh?" Entertainment reporters for the Nashville *Tennessean* covering the event wrote about Manhattanites who immediately asked them about the exotic cultural phenomenon called malls—if they spent inordinate amounts of time in malls and what kinds of stores are in these unusual locations. Many New Yorkers were even surprised that country music had an awards ceremony, asking the reporters, "Isn't that all about people living in trailers and beating their wives? Is it really big enough to have its own awards show?"[1] After the ceremony, *Variety* remarked on the stars' unusual lack of pretension, noting that one obviously surprised winner thanked God, Jesus, and his bus driver. They also noted that, remarkably, no one delivered speeches or thanked her agent.[2]

Suffice it to say, the week preceding the ceremony—called "Country Takes New York City"—was not your typical week in Manhattan. More ten-gallon hats were probably spotted on the subway during these seven days than in the city's entire history. The idea behind the publicity was to get country musicians to appear in obviously urban locales, and reporters waited around to see if it tore a hole in the fabric of the universe. The biggest preliminary event was the Grand Ole Opry's 80th anniversary at Carnegie Hall, marking the first time it had been held there since Minnie Pearl, Ernest Tubb, and Rosalie Allen appeared in 1947 (when Tubb reportedly began by looking around the auditorium and saying, "Boy, this place sure could hold a lot of hay!").

It just so happened that I was planning on being in New York that day, for my first editorial meeting. I was thrilled about going to my publisher's office. While the tourists were taking photos of nearby Radio City Music Hall, I embarrassedly pulled my camera out of my purse and took a picture of my publisher's building. Although it's a towering gray building no one else noticed, it was a beautiful sight to me.

The week before I arrived, my editor e-mailed me to casually ask if I'd like to use one of their extra tickets to the Grand Ole Opry's anniversary celebration at Carnegie Hall. I forced myself to limit the number of exclamation points I used when I e-mailed her back, that, yes, I could be persuaded to go. My exuberance grew when I found out the lineup of stars: Alison Krauss, Martina McBride, Trisha Yearwood, Alan Jackson, Trace Adkins, and Brad Paisley, Charley Pride, Little Jimmy Dickens, Ricky Skaggs, and songwriter Bill Anderson. That evening, as I settled into my seat, I was the happiest person alive.

Vince Gill, the host for the evening, delivered corny and self-deprecating jokes typical of the Grand Ole Opry broadcasts, and the WSM announcer from Nashville delivered a pitch-perfect, soothing narration for the folks listening at home.

Trace Adkins began with a not-so-subtle request for the audience to consider country's universal appeal by singing "Songs About Me"—a ditty about meeting a stranger on the airplane who struck up a conversation after seeing his guitar and saying he wasn't crazy about that hillbilly country music. Then he asked the musician why he'd want to sing that kind of music. The singer says that country music is simply "songs about me and who I am," and then offers the stranger a ticket to his show that night, who reluctantly comes—only to discover that the country songs were all about *his* life as well.

I hadn't heard that song yet, since Philadelphia is not exactly known for its country music scene. But while many people in the audience were experiencing the music for the first time, one of the ladies on the ground floor knew enough to bring a lamp shade to put on her head during Brad Paisley's song "Alcohol." And the songs were gorgeous. Alison Krauss sang Patsy Cline's "He's Got You," a song I used to play on the Huddle House jukebox when little old ladies left me tips in quarters.

Then Vince Gill introduced Alan Jackson as the man who "brought the nation together" after the 9/11 attacks. The hairs on my arms stood up when I thought of all the post–September 11 songs I'd heard from country musicians—none of them were what I'd call unifying. Toby Keith's "Courtesy of the Red, White, and Blue (The Angry American)" had incensed liberals everywhere. In fact, Keith had been scheduled to open ABC's big Fourth of July celebration but was dropped at the last minute at the insistence of Peter Jennings, who was hosting the show. Jennings took particular exception to the lyric "We'll put a boot in your ass. It's the American way," but his snub got Keith even more publicity. (Not that he needed it. In the first week alone, the song sold 338,000 copies.[3]) Reportedly, the commander of the marines fighting in Afghanistan had told Keith, "The country needs this song." And after ABC uninvited him, President Bush personally invited Keith to the White House to play "The Star-Spangled Banner." So I guess the song *was* unifying, but only to a certain segment of America. Keith was very popular with the servicemen and was invited to play on the battleship *New Jersey*, did a tour of U.S. bases in the former Yugoslavia, and instantly became a flashpoint in the culture war.

Vince Gill, however, was not referring to Keith's song but rather to the song President Bush has on his iPod—Alan Jackson's "Where Were You (When the World Stopped Turning)." In this song, Jackson declares he might not know the difference between Iran and Iraq, but he knows Jesus and talks to God.

At the end of the night, the performers came back onstage and broke into a gospel medley that would've driven any Southern church to jealousy, including "I'll Fly Away," "I Saw the Light," and "Will the Circle Be Unbroken?" There was a festive, celebratory spirit in the air, as the whole audience joined in the old familiar songs and clapped to the rhythm. At least, I noticed, they were familiar to some.

It seems Christianity and country music are as inextricable as Scientology and celebrities. If you listen to any country radio station long enough, you'll hear a song about Jesus followed by one about Jack Daniel's—sometimes by the same artist. I never even noticed this musical Christianity when I lived in the South. But as I sat there in Carnegie Hall, the religious references jumped out at me like cinematic sex scenes do when I'm at the movies with my parents. In other words, I immediately noticed them, shifted in my seat, and wondered what everyone else was thinking.

When a black singer got onstage, I was a little relieved. The *New York Times* just days before had printed, "It would be futile to pretend that country pride had nothing in common with white pride."[4] The constant criticism is that country music is redneck music pure and simple, which almost by definition means it's seasoned with racism. Since that whole week purported to show the unity, tradition, and diversity of country music, I thought that Charley Pride would surely allow them to see just how big the country music family is. But when he began to sing, I realized he had chosen an old Hank Williams song about a wooden Indian named "Kaw-Liga." Now liberals usually don't even use the word "Indian." (Remember how my daughter was taught in the Philadelphia public schools to sit "crisscross applesauce" instead of "Indian style"?) Nor do they like to refer to Native American skin color as "red." *The Seattle Times* recently decided to limit the use of the word "Redskins" in their paper even if a team by that name is playing in the area; reporters can use the word once in a story but never in a headline or caption. So when Pride did a rousing rendition of this song— complete with the question "Is it any wonder that his face was red?" and what seemed like several long Indian cries—I couldn't help but notice that the people beside me exchanged worried glances.

Country music has a way of exemplifying all the differences between the red states and the blue in just a few chords—almost every song deals with God, country, family, or the occasional horse. I'll admit the Grand Ole Opry at Carnegie Hall in the middle of New York City created in me a little cognitive dissonance.

Watching Vince Gill sing, my mind drifted back to the days when I was cleaning up his napkins and thanking him for the extra dollars he generously left me on his credit card. I remembered the ache in my feet and the feel of that polyester-blend uniform shirt against my skin while anxiously hoping I could turn a few more tables before the end of the night. My uniform also required both male and female servers to wear neckties, so I remember buying cheap ones from Sears and struggling to tie them in my dorm room. I remember the smell of food that lingered in my hair even after a shower and dreaming of forgetting orders while I slept.

The evening at Carnegie Hall was long, to accommodate all the commercial breaks, so I was able to take my time and breathe in all the details of the night, trying to remember them all—the smell of the program, the feel of the velvet seats, the rhythm of the voices, the butterflies in my stomach. My editor says I have new-authoritis. Too sincere, too pleased, too thrilled at the moments—a euphoria that will fade away like a spray-on tan (and she didn't even *know* I took a picture of her building). But I'm not so sure it's temporary. I get misty-eyed every time I see flags at half-mast, choked up over "The Star-Spangled Banner," and chill bumps when I emerge from Penn Station in New York. That night was quite literally the culmination of years of odd jobs—selling nursing uniforms, answering phones, catering, babysitting, and of course waiting tables—that somehow each propelled me a tad closer to discovering that perhaps I should try writing. So as I sat there next to the editor I'd doubted I'd ever have, I let the words of three thousand people wash over me: "When the shadows of this life have gone, I'll fly away." It was a song I'd sung hundreds of times in church, holding the large, leathery hands of my father. But that night it sounded different—hundreds of miles, several years, and many late-night shifts later.

And I realized the tables had indeed finally turned.

The Liberty Belle

WHEN MY DEAR friend friend Rebecca brought her son up from Kentucky to Philadelphia for a visit, I was more than ready to impress her with my new urban sophistication. Most of my Philly friends figure I just fell off the back of a turnip truck, so I don't disappoint—having inordinate numbers of conversations about guns and grits. But when I'm with my Southern friends, I prefer to impress them with my cosmopolitan ways—which can be accomplished simply by saying, "Let's just jump on the subway," or "I'll take a toasted sesame bagel with Nova Scotia lox, please."

I showed Rebecca around the city in my usual tourist routine: the Visitor Center, the Liberty Bell, and Independence Hall. Even though Rebecca was pregnant at the time, we'd planned a big day of visiting the historical sites. After watching a film on the Revolution, we maneuvered our jogging strollers through the maze of security surrounding the Liberty Bell. The detectors—more sensitive to metal than Tom Cruise is to gay innuendos—went off when my son walked through. After he had repeatedly set the alarm off after various stages of undressing, the guard ushered him through without further inspection, mumbling, "It'd just be cruel to search a three-year-old."

With the geeky bravado of a docent I escorted Rebecca through the Liberty Bell museum (where she made the same observation everyone does, "Wow! It's so . . . small"). I'd been through this exhibit about ten times and could recount every detail of the history of the bell. I knew which Scripture is inscribed on it (Leviticus 25:10), which note it sounds when struck (E flat), and which word is misspelled on it (the word "Pennsylvania" is missing one of the *n*'s in an early spelling).

But no matter how many times I'd been there, I still get choked up every time I read the inscription on the bell, see the tourists snapping pictures, or hear Martin Luther King Jr.'s melodic voice broadcast: "Let freedom ring from every hill and every molehill of Mississippi." Although it's just a hunk of bronze, one and a half million people make a pilgrimage to see it every year—including me. And everyone who visited me. Invariably my guests asked me why, exactly, that bell became famous. You'd think after all these visits, I'd be able to say.

For reasons I still don't quite understand, the old Pennsylvania State House bell has captured the imagination of Americans and has come to symbolize liberty in spite of, or because of, its imperfection. Had the Pennsylvania State House's floors creaked or their toilet clogged up, perhaps we'd think of the abstract notion of liberty as a plank or a plunger. Instead of freedom "ringing" from every mountainside, perhaps it'd be "flushing."

Of course, the Liberty Bell is so popular that it's been used to advertise wars, bread, and life insurance policies. In the 1940s, a comic book even introduced a superhero called the Liberty Belle who was by day a journalist named Libby Lawrence fighting the Nazis with her excellent communication skills. Every time the Liberty Bell in Philadelphia was rung, a tiny bell on her belt buckle rang, imparting adrenaline-enhanced strength. In a small way, I felt like Libby Lawrence. We were both journalists, and— while I wasn't fighting the Nazis—I bravely exposed flaws in the kindergarten curriculum of the Philadelphia public school system. While I didn't have a curve-hugging spandex uniform with a bell on its belt, I did have a wax candle shaped like the Liberty Bell on my dresser.

The one thing I really did have in common with Libby was that I also received inspiration from the Liberty Bell. I walked slowly through the exhibits with Rebecca, enjoying the experience as if it were my first time and not my tenth. By the time we were ready to go on to Independence Hall, I was misty-eyed. Was the sun carved on the back of George Washington's wooden chair rising or setting? Every time I hear old Ben Franklin's assertion that it was indeed rising, it gives me chill bumps. I couldn't wait to walk through the corridors of the state house, imagining the feet that had gone before.

Our three-year-old boys, however, were more interested in engaging in a light-saber battle than in hearing about the less technologically advanced battle we waged against Great Britain. As a courtesy to my pregnant friend who hadn't been through the tour before, I walked the boys back to our building—leaving Rebecca with an empty stroller, the keys to my building, and instructions to have a relaxing day on her own.

I should've remembered to bring her stroller home with me,

because she showed up at 4:45 having forgotten it—not realizing she'd left it chained to a park bench since her son had walked home with me. By the time I jogged several blocks to retrieve it, the rangers were already closing the park. I told the guard I'd forgotten something and promised to hurry. Remarkably, she let me in without the usual security measures, and I quickly found the stroller exactly where Rebecca had told me she'd left it. I darted over, unlocked it, and began rushing out.

Suddenly an authoritative voice stopped me dead in my tracks.

"Stop immediately!" When I came to a halt, I saw that several officers were standing around the stroller in a wide circle around me.

"Is that your stroller?"

"No, sir." As soon as the words escaped my lips, I realized how suspicious I looked, running out of a protected area with an empty stroller. I momentarily considered borrowing a kid from a family of tourists walking by.

"Come over here so I can ask you a few questions." I rolled over to him, preparing to explain the misunderstanding and figuring we'd all laugh about it afterward.

"The bomb squad is on its way over here. We've been here for the past hour guarding this abandoned stroller."

His tone was somewhere between contempt and rage, and my heart started pounding. Faced with the strong arm of the law, I tried all the tactics that have gotten me out of tickets in the South—self-deprecation, charm . . . the truth. I tried to explain how my kids, in spite of my best educational efforts, were more enthusiastic about Darth Maul than George Washington, but the scowl on the officer's face did not vanish.

"This area is protected by the Department of Homeland Security and it is against federal law to leave unattended objects here." He forcefully added for clarity, "You have committed a *crime.*"

My lips began to quiver. This is what happens when I try to hold back emotion; the sheer concentration required to dam my tear ducts causes me to lose control of other body parts. I start to wring my hands. My knee starts bouncing like I'm soothing a baby. I weighed the pros and cons of reminding him it was not my stroller. Instead, I just said repeatedly, "I am so, so sorry" as he lectured me about appropriate behavior in a post-9/11 world. (In this case "I'm sorry" meant "please don't arrest me, sir.") Visions of being dragged away in handcuffs ran through my mind. ("What are you in for?" the prostitute in the corner of the holding cell asks. "Stroller violation," I'd say in an intimidating voice, the prostitute cowering at my capacity for evil.)

I hadn't been lectured like this since scoring two points for the opposing basketball team in junior high. The officer even mocked my Southern accent and angrily explained to me the nuances of living in a big city. "At least that's how we do it here—I don't know where you're from." I resisted the urge to say, "Four blocks to your right."

Then, to add insult to injury, a man in a "John Kerry for President" hat lingered beside us so he could ask the ranger a question. The Democrat looked at me—his eyes full of compassion—as if to say, "This is the America that John Ashcroft created for us." Nonetheless, I appreciated his supportive presence, even though he was probably a pacifist. If the ranger hit me, this man would probably stage a sit-in or write an angry missive to his congressman instead of stepping in, but at least I'd have a witness. And certainly some tourist was getting this on videotape and hoping he could make a buck on the next Rodney King controversy. What if my name became synonymous with national park service brutality? The headlines might scream: "Southern Belle Clubbed at the Liberty Bell." I began composing wry social comments to say in front of the cameras on my way into the courthouse, not wanting to be defined by a lame off-the-cuff comment like "Can't we all just get along?" I'd need something clever and poignant, something that might make me a national star and get me a Cabinet position. As I stood there blinking back tears, I wondered if my status as a pro-America antiterrorist hawk was being challenged. Should I demand that he arrest me?

Then, as suddenly as it had begun, the incident was over. As humiliating as it was, I received only mild threats and some acrid condescension. Presumably, the bomb squad was notified, and I was able to leave freely.

As I walked home, I replayed the day's activities in my head. The lessons I took away from this adventure? First, *never* help forgetful pregnant ladies. Second, if you ever approach a stroller surrounded by angry-looking officers, just look at the ground and keep moving.

I found it poignant that all this happened at Independence Hall. In the Assembly Room of that building, George Washington was appointed commander in chief of the Continental Army in 1775. In 1776, the Declaration of Independence was adopted; in 1787, the U.S. Constitution was drafted; and in 2004, citizens were shoved through metal detectors and the bomb squad was notified because of oblivious pregnant ladies.

We definitely live in a strange world, where our enemies don't helpfully wear black hats and meet us at noon for a show-down. The magnitude and ambiguity of the tension naturally causes discomfort, as we debate the First Amendment and chemical weapons over coffee at playgroups.

Earlier that day, I had read a sign at the Liberty Bell that explained that the bell, like liberty itself, is imperfect and fragile yet has weathered many threats and endured for over two hundred years. Throughout that history, the defense of freedom has demanded citizens to be courageous and vigilant.

What I realize now is that it also requires all of us to be patient, forgiving, and above all, gracious.

Notes

The Blind Date

1. Timothy Noah, "Mister Landslides Neighborhood: Red Versus Blue States Isn't the Half of It," slate.msn.com, April 7, 2004.
2. Source for polling returns: cnn.com/election/2004.

These Y'All's?

1. *Do You Speak American?* "From Sea to Shining Sea," PBS, http://www.pbs.org/speak/seatosea/americanvarieties/southern/sounds/.
2. Moses Velasquez-Manoff, "Y'all's Sprawl: Linguists Study the Spread of a Southern Term," *Houston Chronicle*, February 19, 2005.

Eatin' Good in the Neighborhood

1. David Brooks, "One Nation, Slightly Divisible," *The Atlantic*, December 2001.
2. Tom Curry, "Is Democrats' Solution on the Menu at Applebee's?" MSNBC, November 10, 2004.
3. Michael Graham, "You Are What You Eat," *The Free Times*.

The Real Rainbow Coalition

1. "Godless Hollywood? Bible Belt? New Research Exploring Faith in America's Largest Markets Produces Surprise," the Barna Group, www.barna.org. Barna Update, August 23, 2005. Used by permission.

Cheese and Rice

1. J. J. Goldberg, the editor of *The Forward*, as quoted by Lloyd Grove in the New York *Daily News*, November 12, 2004. http://www.nydailynews.com/front/story/252115p-215740c .html.

Wanna Coke?

1. "Standard American English," PBS, *Do You Speak American?* www.pbs.org/speak/seatosea/standardamerican.
2. "American Dialects," extended version of an article published in *Let's Go USA 2004*, Bert Vaux, Harvard University, July 2003.
3. Scott Leith, "In the South, a 'Coke' Could Be a Pepsi," *The Atlanta Journal-Constitution*, January 27, 2005.
4. Ron Butters, a professor of linguistics, as quoted by Bill Hendrick, "It's Soooooo New," *The Atlanta Journal-Constitution*, June 17, 2004.
5. Ken Gewertz, "Standing on Line at the Bubbler with a Hoagie in My Hand: Bert Vaux Maps America's Dialects," *Harvard Gazette*, December 12, 2002. www.harvard.edu/gazette/2002/12.12/ 08-vaux.html.
6. Carmen Fought, "Are Dialects Fading?" *Do You Speak American?* www.pbs.org/speak/seatosea.

The Real Curse of the Jade Scorpion

1. David Brooks, "One Nation, Slightly Divisible," *The Atlantic*, December 2001.
2. Brooks, ibid.
3. Gary Trudeau's August 26, 2001, *Doonesbury* comic strip featured an invisible George W. Bush being told about his ranking on the presidential IQ ladder by an underling.
4. Matthew Norman, "Diary," *The Guardian*, July 19, 2001; *The Southland Times*, August 7, 2001. Urban Legends Reference Pages, "Presidential IQ," http://www.snopes.com/inboxer/hoaxes/presiq.htm.
5. Michael Kranish, "Yale Grades Portray Kerry as a Lackluster Student," *The Boston Globe*, June 7, 2005.
6. Steve Sailer, "Bush's Brain," *The American Conservative*, December 6, 2004, http://www.amconmag.com/2004_12_06.

The Exhausted American

1. David Brooks, "One Nation, Slightly Divisible," *The Atlantic*, December 2001.
2. Susan Sontag, "Talk of the Town," *The New Yorker*, September 24, 2001.
3. Katha Pollitt, "Put Out No Flags," *The Nation*, October 8, 2001.
4. "FIRE Coalition Shatters Window Display Censorship Policy at University of Alabama," Foundation for Individual Rights in Education, October 3, 2003, http://www.thefire.org/index.php/article/176.html.
5. Partial transcript of comments from the September 13, 2001, telecast of *The 700 Club*, available at http://archives.cnn.com/2001/US/09/14/Falwell.apology/.

6. Associated Press, "Marine's Family Upset Official Came to Funeral," July 25, 2005; available at http://www.cnn.com/2005/
   US/07/25/funeral.apology.ap/index.html.

Turning Tables

1. Ryan Underwood, "The Sites and Sounds of Country in New
   York," *The Tennessean*, November 15, 2005.
2. Elizabeth Guider, "Urban Setting for the CMAs," *Variety*, November 21, 2005, http://www.variety.com/vstory/VR1117933290?
   categoryid=38&cs=1&query=urban+and+setting &display=u.
3. John Sutherland, "Return of the Ugly American," *The Guardian*,
   August 26, 2002, http://www.guardian.co.uk/Columnists/
   Column/0,5673,780739,00.html.
4. Kelefa Sanneh, "Country Music? Whose Country?" *New York
   Times*, November 11, 2005.